Keyboarding Course

Lessons 1-25

20e

Susie H. VanHuss
Ph.D., Distinguished Professor Emeritus,
University of South Carolina

Connie M. Forde
Ph.D., Mississippi State University

Donna L. Woo
Cypress College, California

Vicki R. Robertson
Southwest Tennessee Community College

COLLEGE KEYBOARDING

CENGAGE

Australia • Brazil • Mexico • Singapore • United Kingdom • United States

CENGAGE

College Keyboarding: Keyboarding Course Lessons 1-25, **Twentieth Edition**
Susie H. VanHuss, Connie M. Forde, Donna L. Woo, Vicki R. Robertson

SVP, GM Skills & Global Product Management: Dawn Gerrain

Product Director: Kathleen McMahon

Product Team Manager: Elinor W. Gregory

Product Manager: Amanda Lyons

Senior Director, Development: Marah Bellegarde

Senior Product Development Manager: Larry Main

Senior Content Developer: Anne Orgren

Product Assistant: Cara Suriyamongkol

Vice President, Marketing Services: Jennifer Ann Baker

Marketing Director: Michele McTighe

Senior Production Director: Wendy Troeger

Production Director: Patty Stephan

Senior Content Project Manager: Brooke Greenhouse

Senior Designer: Diana Graham

Cover image(s): en-owai/Shutterstock.com

© 2017, 2014 Cengage Learning, Inc.

ALL RIGHTS RESERVED. No part of this work covered by the copyright herein may be reproduced or distributed in any form or by any means, except as permitted by U.S. copyright law, without the prior written permission of the copyright owner.

All screenshots, unless otherwise noted, are from Microsoft Corporation. Microsoft® is a registered trademark of the Microsoft Corporation.

Key reach images: © Cengage Learning, Cengage Learning/Bill Smith Group/Sam Kolich

Keyboard images: ©Cengage Learning

> For product information and technology assistance, contact us at
> **Cengage Customer & Sales Support, 1-800-354-9706**
> **or support.cengage.com.**
>
> For permission to use material from this text or product, submit all requests online at **www.cengage.com/permissions.**

Library of Congress Control Number: 2016934320

ISBN: 978-1-337-10325-1

Cengage
20 Channel Street
Boston, MA 02210
USA

Cengage is a leading provider of customized learning solutions with employees residing in nearly 40 different countries and sales in more than 125 countries around the world. Find your local representative at: **www.cengage.com.**

Cengage products are represented in Canada by Nelson Education, Ltd.

To learn more about Cengage platforms and services, register or access your online learning solution, or purchase materials for your course, visit **www.cengage.com.**

Notice to the Reader

Publisher does not warrant or guarantee any of the products described herein or perform any independent analysis in connection with any of the product information contained herein. Publisher does not assume, and expressly disclaims, any obligation to obtain and include information other than that provided to it by the manufacturer. The reader is expressly warned to consider and adopt all safety precautions that might be indicated by the activities described herein and to avoid all potential hazards. By following the instructions contained herein, the reader willingly assumes all risks in connection with such instructions. The publisher makes no representations or warranties of any kind, including but not limited to, the warranties of fitness for particular purpose or merchantability, nor are any such representations implied with respect to the material set forth herein, and the publisher takes no responsibility with respect to such material. The publisher shall not be liable for any special, consequential, or exemplary damages resulting, in whole or part, from the readers' use of, or reliance upon, this material.

Printed in the United States of America
Print Number: 05   Print Year: 2019

Contents

The Power of Keyboarding..........iv
Know Your Computer vii
Keyboarding Assessment/
Placement viii

LEVEL 1
Developing Keyboarding Skill

Module 1: Alphabetic Keys

1	Home Row, Space Bar, Enter, I	1-2
1R	Review................	1-6
2	E and N	1-7
3	Review................	1-9
4	Left Shift, H, T, Period ..	1-11
4R	Review................	1-13
5	R, Right Shift, C, O	1-14
5R	Review................	1-16
6	W, Comma, B, P	1-17
7	Review................	1-19
8	G, Question Mark, X, U .	1-21
8R	Review................	1-23
9	Q, M, V, Apostrophe	1-24
9R	Review................	1-26
10	Z, Y, Quotation Mark, Tab	1-27
11	Review................	1-29
12	Review................	1-31
13	Review................	1-33

Skill Builder 1 1-35

Module 2: Figure and Symbol Keys

14	1 and 8	1-40
15	5 and 0	1-42
16	2 and 7	1-44
17	4 and 9	1-46
18	3 and 6	1-48
18R	Review................	1-50
19	$ and - (hyphen)........	1-51
20	# and /	1-53
21	% and !	1-55
22	(and) and Backspace Key....................	1-57
23	& and : (colon), Proofreaders' Marks....	1-59
24	Other Symbols	1-61
24R	Review................	1-63
25	Assessment.............	1-64

Skill Builder 2 1-66
Skill Builder 3 1-72
Numeric Keypad 1-77

LEVEL 1a
Applying Keyboarding Skill

Word Processing 1a-2
Communication Skills...... 1a-11
Web-Based Computing:
Internet, Cloud, and
Social Media.............. 1a-23
Prepare for Your Future ... 1a-27

LEVEL 1b
Technology and You

Digital Citizenship 1b-2
Keyboarding—Bridge
to Today's Technology 1b-4
Technology and Your
Health 1b-5

Appendix A:
Windows 10 .... REF1
Appendix B:
File Management............ REF5
Appendix C:
Reference Guide REF10
Index REF15

The Power of Keyboarding... Starts Here!

LEARN . . . DISCOVER

Touch Keyboarding

Communication Skills

Windows 10 Basics

Discover the power of *College Keyboarding, 20th edition* print and digital solutions.

College Keyboarding, 20e, combines easy-to-use tools with a proven track record of ensuring classroom and workplace success.

Keyboarding in Skills Assessment Manager (SAM) provides the tools to master document skills for use in school, career, and personal situations.

NEW to This Edition

- Coverage of *Windows 10*
- Correlation with the web-based *Skills Assessment Manager (SAM)* to build, apply, and assess skills
- Deletion of KPDO references and updated instructions in the print book so that the book is not dependent on KPDO
- Updated Know Your Computer section reflecting changes in computer hardware and software
- Updated drill lines to conform to the key presentation sequence
- New standard plans in the Skill Builders for using timed writings, building speed, and improving accuracy; updated instructions in drills and timed writings to enable students to apply these plans
- Number Expression moved to Lessons 1–55 book

Meet SAM (Skills Assessment Manager)

SAM's online learning environments enable students to learn *Microsoft Office* and computer concepts essential to academic and career success. Students observe and practice, then apply their skills in the live application. Autograded assignments save time and energy.

For the 20th edition of *College Keyboarding*, SAM replaces KPDO as an optional digital companion to the print text. With SAM, the keying drills, timed writings, skill buildings, and other activities can be completed and submitted online. If your course is using SAM, visit http://sam.cengage.com to find out more about how to use SAM with this textbook.

Ready, Set, Key!

The keys to success include carefully designed lessons and reliable, dependable, easy-to-use technology tools.

An abundance of crafted exercises keep lessons fun and help build a strong foundation.

Skill Building Drills and Timed Writings

Build confidence and success through keying exercises and timed writings.

Workplace Success

Learn how to survive and thrive in the workplace with tips provided in Workplace Success boxes.

Skill Builders

Strengthen your techniques and accuracy as well as build speed through extra practice with Skill Builders at the end of each module.

Communication Activities

Build skills in proofreading, composition, and more through practicing communication activities.

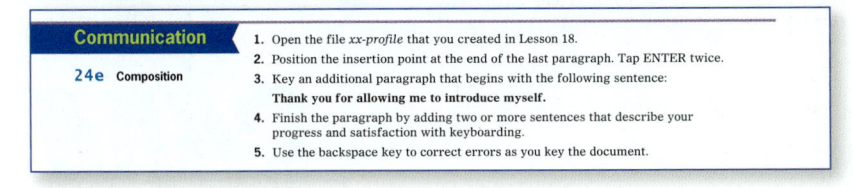

THE POWER OF KEYBOARDING... STARTS HERE!

Powerful Tools . . . Working for You

College Keyboarding 20e provides the tools students need to develop expertise in keyboarding, document formatting, and essential word processing skills using *Microsoft Word 2016*.

ISBN 9781337103251 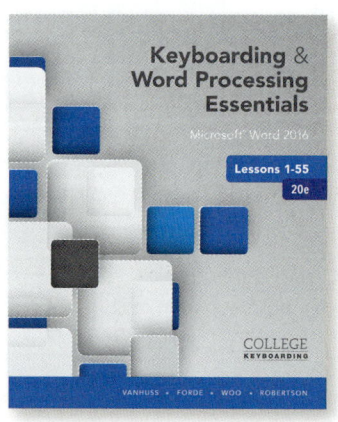   ISBN 9781337103022 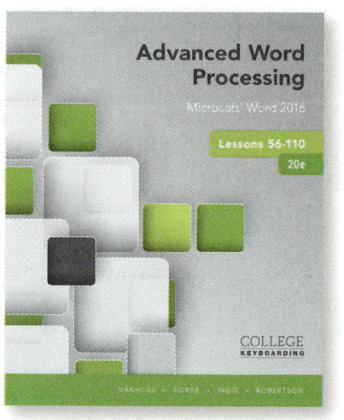   ISBN 9781337103268    ISBN 9781337103275

Supplemental Resources

Instructor Companion Site

A robust instructor companion website provides the materials you need to teach this course, including an instructor's manual; tests; solution files; syllabus; Communication Skills pretests, post-tests, and references; and more. To access the instructor companion site, sign in to login.cengage.com and add this text to your instructor dashboard.

Student Companion Site

The data files needed to complete this text's activities are found on the free student companion website for this text. To access the student companion site, visit login.cengage.com and search for this text.

Keyboarding in Skills Assessment Manager (SAM)

For the 20th edition of *College Keyboarding*, SAM replaces KPDO as an optional digital companion to the print text. With SAM, the keying drills, timed writings, skill buildings, and other activities can be completed and submitted online.

Instructors may teach the course using the print book only, the print book plus SAM, or SAM only. If your course is using SAM, visit http://sam.cengage.com to find out more about how to use SAM with this textbook. To purchase SAM with a print textbook, speak to your Cengage Learning Consultant.

THE POWER OF KEYBOARDING... STARTS HERE!

Know Your Computer

All-in-One Computer
Monitor and Processor Combined
Keyboard and Mouse Separate

Laptop Computer
Monitor, Processor, Keyboard, and Mouse Combined

Desktop Computer
Monitor, Processor, Keyboard, and Mouse Separate

Keys to Enter/Format Text

1. **Alphanumeric**—letters, numbers, and symbols.
2. **Tab**—positions text at fixed points.
3. **Caps Lock**—capitalizes all letters.
4. **Shift key**—capitalizes single letter; keys symbols.
5. **Space bar**—inserts space in text.
6. **Enter**—moves insertion point down to next line.
7. **Backspace**—deletes text to left of insertion point.
8. **Delete**—removes text to right of insertion point.
9. **Insert**—adds text or activates typeover.
10. **Numeric keypad**—numbers.

Keys to Execute Commands or Navigate

(Command keys often are used with other keys and vary with software.)

11. **Function (F1–F12) keys**
12. **Esc (Escape)**—cancel; stops action.
13. **Ctrl (Control)**
14. **Windows key**—displays Start menu and executes other commands.
15. **Alt (Alternate)**
16. **Arrow keys**—moves insertion point up, down, left, or right.
17. **Navigation keys**—Home, End, Page Up, and Page Down.

KNOW YOUR COMPUTER

vii

Keyboarding Assessment/Placement

Warmup

Key the paragraph using wordwrap (do not tap ENTER at the end of lines). Repeat if desired.

Good keyboarding skills are essential for almost all careers today. The time spent learning to key quickly and accurately is time well spent. Use good posture and good techniques to get you started on the right track. Then work diligently to achieve your speed and accuracy goals. Good keyboarding skills will save you time in preparing assignments for all of your classes. Also your work will impress your instructors.

LA ALL LETTERS

Timed Writing

1. Take a 3' timed writing; use wordwrap (do not tap ENTER at the end of lines).
2. Tap TAB to begin.
3. Take a second 3' timed writing.

Note:
1' = 1 minute
30" = 30 seconds

	gwam	1'	3'
Learning to key is just the first step toward developing a very		13	4
meaningful career skill. The next step is to build both speed and		26	9
accuracy. With basic keyboarding skills, you will be able to present		39	13
information in an attractive format that is quite easy to read. You will		54	18
also be able to develop your communication skills at the same time.		67	22
The next big step is to learn word processing. The software		12	26
most often used in business organizations is Word, which is much		25	31
more sophisticated than the basic word processor you used for		37	35
your warmup. With Word you will be able to create attractive		49	39
letters, memos, reports, and many other types of documents used		61	43
in business.		64	44
One of the exciting things about working diligently to develop		12	48
a skill is that you have the opportunity to set very specific goals		26	52
and challenge yourself to meet them. Nothing is more motivating		38	56
than being able to accomplish the goals that we set for ourselves.		52	61
The incremental goals that you meet each day will result in major		65	65
progress by the end of the course.		71	67

1' | 1 | 2 | 3 | 4 | 5 | 6 | 7 | 8 | 9 | 10 | 11 | 12 |
3' | | 1 | | 2 | | 3 | | 4 |

KEYBOARDING ASSESSMENT/PLACEMENT

LEVEL 1

Developing Keyboarding Skill

Learning Outcomes

Keyboarding
+ Key the alphabetic and numeric keys by touch.
+ Develop good keyboarding techniques.
+ Key fluently—at least 25 words per minute.
+ Develop reasonable accuracy.

Communication Skills
+ Develop proofreading skills.
+ Apply proofreaders' marks and revise text.

SET UP YOUR WORK ENVIRONMENT

The setup depends on the physical size of the individual and the type of computer being used.

Laptops

Laptop and tablet computers are not designed ergonomically. They are fine for occasional use but are not as effective for extensive computer use. Laptops used extensively are best set up with a docking station which allows the user to plug in a separate monitor and/or a separate keyboard. The laptop can then be set up in the same manner that a desktop computer is set up.

Desktop Computers

The position of the monitor, keyboard, mouse, and chair are important. A few guides to follow:

- Position the screen so that the top is at about eye level and about arm's length from the user. Avoid glare from windows if possible. Increase the size of the text and icons on the screen if necessary.
- The keyboard tray should be positioned so that it is about two inches above your thighs and your arms are parallel to the floor.
- The mouse should be positioned close to the keyboard.
- Adjust the chair to a comfortable position.

POSITION THE USER APPROPRIATELY

Correct posture and hand position are important. Moving around and frequent breaks are also important. Exercises to relax your eyes and strengthen your fingers and muscles are also helpful.

- Sit upright in the chair and face the computer; feet should be flat on the floor.
- Arms should be parallel to the floor and wrists straight.
- Position the arms close to the body.
- User position should be such that extended reaching is not necessary.

MODULE 1

Alphabetic Keys

LEARNING OUTCOMES

Lessons 1–10   *Alphabetic and Basic Punctuation Keys*

Lessons 11–13   *Review*

- Key the alphabetic keys by touch.
- Key using proper techniques.
- Key at a rate of 14 *gwam* or more.

Lesson 1   Home Row, Space Bar, Enter, I

Keyboarding   *A Wise Investment Now and For Your Career*

As you begin your keyboarding course, think about these two questions:

1. Why is keyboarding a great investment?

The ability to key rapidly and accurately is a lifelong skill. Instructors in virtually all courses expect you to submit papers and other assignments that have been keyed accurately and formatted attractively. Good keyboarding skills will result in time saved and will also give you a competitive advantage in courses such as *Word*, *Excel*, and *PowerPoint* as well as in many other courses, part-time jobs, and ultimately your career.

2. How can I get the best return on my investment?

Keyboarding is a psychomotor skill that requires muscle memory development with corrective drills and practice just as a pianist preparing for a concert or an athlete preparing for a sporting event has to develop basic skills. Your ultimate success in keying effectively is determined by the keyreach techniques you develop. You build muscle memory by reinforcing correct reaches over and over. Position is the constant point of reference for successful typists. Your textbook, software, and instructor will serve as your coach in developing the correct:

- Body position
- Finger position
- Wrist position
- Eyes position on screen/copy

Technology and Your Health

YOU ARE IN CHARGE!

Medical self-management is a very popular concept in the prevention, treatment, and control of diseases such as chronic pain, diabetes, asthma, stress, high blood pressure, and many others. Patients can be trained to prevent, treat, and control many of the symptoms and problems caused by these diseases. In fact, some patients become more effective at managing their disease than their medical staff. A number of health issues may be associated with the use of technology, but nobody is in a better position to prevent and manage these issues than you are. The most important concept to remember is that prevention is far more effective than curing health issues.

TECHNOLOGY HEALTH ISSUES

Many computer users are quick to blame the monitor, keyboard, and mouse for eye strain, repetitive stress injuries (RSIs), cumulative trauma disorders (CTDs), and carpal tunnel syndrome (CTS). The appropriate question is: Is the technology the cause of the problems, or is the real culprit the way the technology is set up and used?

Which of the three extensive computer users pictured here is least likely to experience some of the issues listed above?

The user in the center is least likely to experience some of the issues listed above for several reasons:

- He is the only one not using a laptop. Laptops are difficult to position comfortably because the screen and keyboard are both attached. With a laptop, typically the screen is too low or the keyboard is too high.
- With the desktop computer, the screen is large and is positioned at a comfortable height and distance; the keyboard is at the correct height, and the mouse is next to it.
- The user's posture, hand, and arm position are correct.
- The user on the left is likely to have difficulty reading the screen because of the distance, the upward tilt, and the glare. The forward-leaning posture with keyboard too far back as well as poor hand and wrist position will likely lead to fatigue and poor results.
- The user on the right is using a laptop that is placed on an angle on the corner of the desk with the screen toward the window creating glare. The user is leaning to his left, resting on his left arm. The right arm is resting on the desk.

Note the proper way to set up your work environment on the next page, and critique the pictures again.

| STANDARD PLAN | For Learning New Keyreaches |

1. Find the new key on the illustrated keyboard. Then find it on your keyboard.
2. Watch your finger make the reach to the new key a few times. Keep other fingers curved in home position. For an upward reach, straighten the finger slightly; for a down reach, curve the finger a bit more.
3. Use these directions for learning all new keyreaches.

New Keys

1a Learn Home Row

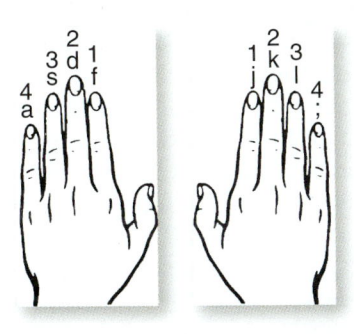

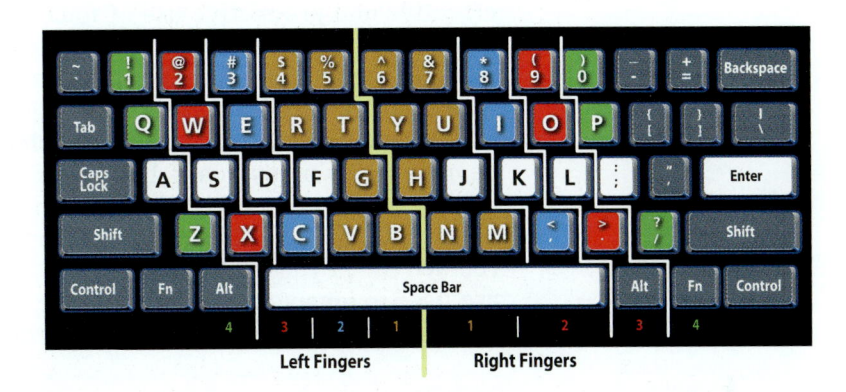

HOME-ROW POSITION

1. Drop your hands to your side. Allow your fingers to curve naturally. Maintain this curve as you key.
2. Lightly place your left fingers over the **a s d f** and the right fingers over the **j k l ;**. You will feel a raised element on the **f** and **j** keys, which will help you keep your fingers on the home-row position. You are now in home-row position.

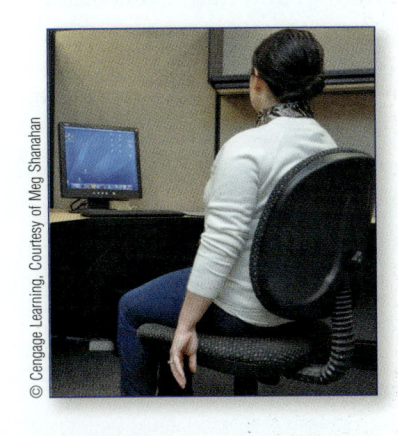

Note the curve of your fingers when your arms are hanging loosely at your side. Maintain this same curve when you place your hands on the home row.

LESSON 1   HOME ROW, SPACE BAR, ENTER, I   MODULE 1   1-3

Keyboarding—Bridge to Today's Technology

WHO NEEDS A KEYBOARD WITH TODAY'S TECHNOLOGY?

This question is frequently asked and framed in many ways. Often it takes the form of: Are keyboarding skills still valid and necessary with touch, pen, and voice technology available?

The most frequent answer to the question is that everyone who needs a computer in their lives or in their jobs needs keyboarding skill. It is simply a prerequisite for effective and productive use of today's technology. Note the keywords—effective and productive use. Individuals who do not have effective touch keyboarding skills are at a significant disadvantage using today's technology. It is clear that the self-taught hunt-and-peck system is neither adequate nor acceptable. Voice technology, pen technology, the mouse, and touch technology have been in existence for a number of years and, for many years, have been predicted to replace keyboarding skill. Yet, market penetration for those skills in business offices is negligible. Touch technology has proliferated on mobile devices primarily for navigation. However, it cannot replace the keyboard for keying the documents, spreadsheets, or presentations that are used extensively in business. The need for keyboarding skills continues to flourish, and the investment in developing keyboarding skills continues to be a wise one.

WHAT JOBS REQUIRE COMPUTERS (AND THUS KEYBOARDING SKILLS)?

A number of years ago, keyboarding skills were often thought of as clerical skills. Today, most estimates show that keyboarding skills are communication and technical skills used in more than 90 percent of all jobs. Careers that are enhanced significantly by keyboarding skills include medical, legal, business, journalism, scientific, engineering, teaching, and numerous other fields.

Developing excellent keyboarding techniques and skills is necessary to use computers effectively in the workplace.

The keyboard is likely to be the primary input device for computers for many years to come. Learn to use it effectively!

KEYBOARDING—BRIDGE TO TODAY'S TECHNOLOGY

1b-4

1b Learn Space Bar and ENTER

SPACE BAR AND ENTER

Tap the Space Bar, located at the bottom of the keyboard, with a down-and-in motion of the right thumb to space between words.

Enter Reach with the fourth (little) finger of the right hand to ENTER. Tap it to return the insertion point to the left margin. This action creates a **hard return**. Use a hard return at the end of all drill lines. Quickly return to home position (over ;).

1c Master New Keys

Key each line once. Tap ENTER at the end of each line.

```
 1  j   jj  f   ff  k   kk  d   dd  l   ll  s   ss  ;   ;;  a   aa  jkl;  fdsa
 2  a   aa  ;   ;;  s   ss  l   ll  d   dd  k   kk  f   ff  j   jj  fdsa  jkl;

 3  ff  jj  ff  jj  fj  fj  fj  dd  kk  dd  kk  dk  dk  dk
 4  ss  ll  ss  ll  sl  sl  sl  aa  ;;  aa  ;;  a;  a;  a;
 5  fj  fj  dk  dk  sl  sl  a;  fjdk  sla;  fjkd  ls;a
 6  fff  jjj  fjf  fff  jjj  fjf  fjf  jfj  jfj  fjf
 7  ddd  kkk  dkd  ddd  kkk  dkd  dkd  kdk  kdk  dkd
 8  sss  lll  sls  sss  lll  sls  sls  lsl  lsl  sls
 9  aaa  ;;;  a;a  aaa  ;;;  a;a  a;a  ;a;  ;a;  a;a
10  f   j   d   k   s   l   a   ;   ;   a   l   s   k   d   j   f
11  ff  jj  dd  kk  ss  ll  aa  ;;  jj  ff  kk  dd  ll  ss  aa  ;;
12  fff  jjj  ddd  kkk  sss  lll  aaa  jjj  ;;;  fjdk  sla;
```

> Keep your eyes on the textbook as you key each line.

1d Improve Keystroking

Key each line once. Tap ENTER at the end of each line.

```
13  a   a;  al  ak  aj  s   s;  sl  sk  sj  d   d;  dl  dk  dj
14  j   ja  js  jd  jf  k   ka  ks  kd  kf  l   la  ls  ld  lf
15  a;  sl  a;sl  dkfj  a;sl  dkfj  a;sl  dkfj  asdf  jk
16  a;  sl  a;sl  dk  fj  dkfj  a;sl  dkfj  fjdk  a;a
17  f   ff  j   jj  d   dd  k   kk  s   ss  l   ll  a   aa  ;   ;;  fj
18  afj;  a   s   d   f   j   k   l   ;   asdf  jkl;  fdsa  jkl;
```

LESSON 1 HOME ROW, SPACE BAR, ENTER, I   MODULE 1   1-4

Plagiarism. Copyright laws protect material from unauthorized use. Request permission before using copyrighted materials. It is not acceptable to copy information from the Internet without properly documenting the source of the information and giving the writer proper credit. Software is available to check a paper and quickly determine if it has been plagiarized.

Piracy. Downloading of music, games, and movies and making copies of software without permission are illegal.

SAFETY

Privacy. Protecting private information and company proprietary information are key safety concerns. Protect your information and/or your company's information by using up-to-date antivirus software, antispyware, and firewalls.

Identity theft. Unauthorized persons may obtain information such as your Social Security number or credit card information and use it for criminal purposes. Posting private information on social networks can have serious negative consequences as shown in the following examples.

- Posting pictures of vacation sites and travel information alerted criminals that the family was away and their home was robbed.
- Posting pictures of children on the Internet and address information in other locations attracted predators to the home.
- Unprofessional information and pictures on a social network were viewed by a potential employer causing the person not to be hired. Many employers check out potential employees on social networks before hiring them.
- Negative information posted about a person's supervisor and company was viewed by company executives.

CIVILITY

Courtesy and good manners when posting information, sending emails, participating in a chat room, blogging, or posting on a social media site are always appropriate. The following tips are examples of good *netiquette*.

- Consider anything you post to be public information. Many people use technology to deliver messages that they would never send in a face-to-face situation.
- Use appropriate, non-offensive language and be sensitive to cultural issues.
- Avoid inflammatory messages and messages keyed in all capital letters.
- Be helpful to people who have less technical expertise than you do. They may have great ideas even though they are not technically savvy.
- Avoid texting and checking and sending emails, and place cell phones on vibrate during meetings and dining.

DIGITAL CITIZENSHIP

1e i

i Reach *up* with *right second* finger.

19 i ik ik ik is is id id if if ill i ail did kid lid
20 i ik aid ail did kid lid lids kids ill aid did ilk
21 id aid aids laid said ids lid skids kiss disk dial

Use good posture; back and body erect; feet flat on the floor.

1f Master New Keys

i

22 id aid ail fail sail jail ails slid dill sill fill
23 aid lads; if a kid is; a salad lid; kiss a sad dad
24 as ad all ask jak lad fad said ill kill fall disks
25 is all sad lass a lid; is silk; silk disk; dad is;

1g Build Skill

26 as as ask ask ad ad lad lad all all fall fall asks
27 as asks did disk ail fail sail ails jail sill silk
28 ask dad; dads said; is disk; kiss a lad; salad lid
29 fill a sail; aid a lad; is silk; if a dial; a jail
30 is a disk; dads said; did fall ill; if a lass did;

! WORKPLACE SUCCESS

Keyboarding: The Survival Skill

Keyboarding is a valuable and necessary skill for everyone in this technological world. It is an expected tool for effective communication throughout one's life.

Students who resort to "hunting and pecking" to key their school assignments are constantly searching for the correct letter on the keyboard. Frustration abounds for students who wish to key their research reports into the computer but do not have the touch keyboarding skills required to accomplish the task quickly and proficiently. Students who can key by touch are much more relaxed because they can keep their eyes on the screen and concentrate on text editing and composing.

LESSON 1 HOME ROW, SPACE BAR, ENTER, I

Digital Citizenship

OVERVIEW

One search using a popular search engine and *digital citizenship* as keywords produced over three million results. A quick survey of the list of documents indicated that digital citizenship is a popular, if not required, topic in the curricula of K–12 schools. Many of the documents focused on digital citizenship research by Dr. Mike Ribble, on the framework developed by the Partnership for 21st Century Skills, and on the International Society for Technology in Education Standards for Students. A relatively small percentage of the documents listed referred to collegiate education or business and industry.

This article focuses on effective digital citizenship from four perspectives that can affect your career.

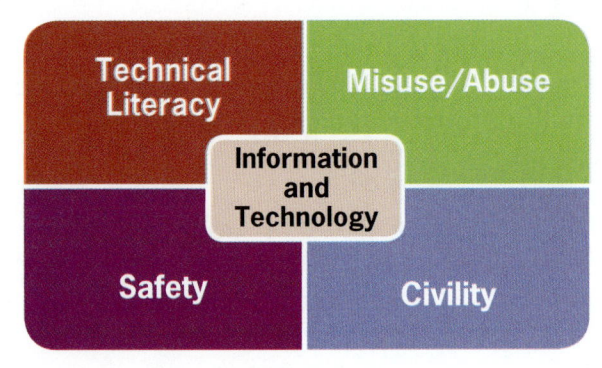

TECHNICAL LITERACY

Understanding how the Internet, social media applications, and other digital tools work enables you to use these tools creatively, responsibly, and safely. Technology is constantly evolving; things learned today can be outdated in a very short time. Therefore, continual learning is the only way to keep up with technology. Protecting your (or your company's) computer, network, and information from unauthorized access is critical. Many students and young employees who have grown up using all types of technology may be more technically savvy than their instructors or their managers. However, they often do not have the social skills and business savvy to be effective in using digital tools.

MISUSE/ABUSE

The Internet is a vast collection of information that can be accessed easily and at little or no cost. However, just because information has been posted on the Internet does not mean that it is accurate or valid.

Information Verification. Information should be analyzed carefully to determine the credibility of the writer, the source of the information, the accuracy of details, knowledge of the literature, and the currency of the information before relying on that information.

Lesson 1R Review

Warmup *Lesson 1Ra Warmup*

Fingers curved and upright

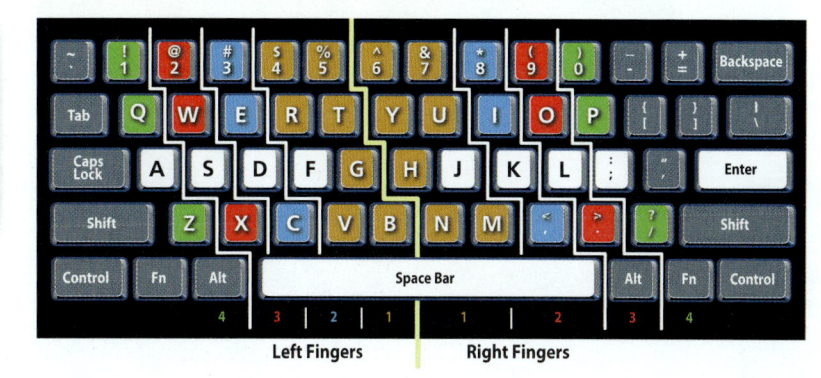

Left Fingers   Right Fingers

```
1  ff dd ss aa ff dd ss aa jj kk ll ;; fj dk sl a; a;
2  fj dk sla; fjdk sla; a;sl dkfj fjdk sla; fjdk sla;
3  aa ss dd ff jj kk ll ;; aa ss dd ff jj kk ll ;; a;
4  if a; as is; kids did; ask a sad lad; if a lass is
```

Skill Building

1Rb Improve Techniques

Key each line once.

Move fingers without moving your hands; eyes on textbook.

```
5  f  j  fjf  jj  fj  fj  jf  dd  kk  dd  kk  dk  dk  dk
6  s  ;  s;s  ;;  s;  s;  s;  aa  ;;  aa  ;;  a;  a;  a;
7  fj  dk  sl  a;  fjdk  sla;  jfkd  lsa;  ;a  ;a  ;s
8  f  j  fjf  d  k  dkd  s  l  sls  a  ;  fj  dk  sl  a;a
9  a;  al  aka  j  s  s;  sl  sk  sj  d  d;  dl  dk  djd
10 ja  js  jd  jf  k  ka  ks  kd  kf  l  la  ls  ld  lfl
```

1Rc Improve Keystroking

```
11 f fa fad s sa sad f fa fall fall l la lad s sa sad
12 a as ask a ad add j ja jak f fa fall; ask; add jak
13 ik ki ki ik is if id il ij ia ij ik is if ji id ia
14 is il ill sill dill fill sid lid ail lid slid jail
15 if is il kid kids ill kid if kids; if a kid is ill
```

LEVEL **1b**

Technology and You

Learning Outcomes

Digital Citizenship

+ To enhance technical literacy.
+ To learn appropriate Internet behavior and improve digital civility.
+ To learn how to prevent Internet misuse and abuse.
+ To learns ways to improve Internet safety.

Keyboarding – Bridge to Today's Technology

+ To understand the importance of keyboarding skills in overall technical competency.
+ To be aware of the careers that require computer and keyboarding skills.

Technology and Your Health

+ To learn how to set up technology to avoid health issues, such as eye strain, repetitive stress injuries, and carpal tunnel syndrome.
+ To learn how to set up the work environment to avoid health issues.
+ To learn the correct posture and hand position to avoid health issues.

Lesson 2 E and N

Warmup   Lesson 2a Warmup

1 ff dd ss aa ff dd ss aa jj kk ll ;; fj dk sl a; a;
2 fj dk sl a; fjdk sla; a;sl dkfj dk sl a; fjdk sla;
3 aa ss dd ff jj kk ll ;; aa ss dd ff jj kk ll ;; a;
4 if a; as is; kids did; ask a sad lad; if a lass is

New Keys

2b   e and n

e Reach *up* with *left second* finger.

n Reach *down* with *right first* finger.

e

5 e ed ed led led lea lea ale ale elf elf eke eke ed
6 e el el eel els elk elk lea leak ale kale led jell
7 e ale kale lea leak fee feel lea lead elf self eke

n

8 n nj nj an an and and fan fan and kin din fin land
9 n an fan in fin and land sand din fans sank an sin
10 n in ink sink inn kin skin an and land in din dink

2c   All Reaches Learned

11 den end fen ken dean dens ales fend fens keen knee
12 if in need; feel ill; as an end; a lad and a lass;
13 and sand; a keen idea; as a sail sank; is in jail;
14 an idea; an end; a lake; a nail; a jade; a dean is

LESSON 2 E AND N   MODULE 1   1-7

> **TIP**
>
> If you have a work schedule conflict, ask your instructor to approve your participation by telephone. All members must participate in the discussion.

Part III, Option 1 – Team Meeting and Discussion (Team Option)

1. Meet with your team and discuss the answers each of you obtained. If you are in the same location, use a face-to-face team meeting. If you are distance education students meeting in different locations, use a chat or discussion option.
2. List all soft skills recommended by the individuals interviewed.
3. Reach a consensus on what the team thinks are the five most important soft skills recommended by the individuals interviewed. (Do not vote—discuss until you agree on the important soft skills.)

Part III, Option 2 – Research Soft Skills (Individual Option)

1. Locate and find three current articles on soft skills needed most by employees. Make sure they come from reliable sources. Key the names and source information for the articles. Write a sentence or two on why you believe each source is reliable.
2. Compare the soft skills from your interview notes to those recommended in the three articles.
3. Prepare a list of at least ten important soft skills from your interview and the articles.
4. Review them carefully and list the five soft skills that you think are most important for your career.

Part IV – Soft Skills Assessment (Required for Both Teams and Individuals)

1. Use a 1 to 5 scale with 5 being the highest (your strengths) and 1 being the lowest (your weaknesses) to evaluate yourself honestly on the five most important soft skills listed in Part III, Option 1 or 2.
2. List things that you can do to improve on the two skills that were rated lowest in item 1 above. Use the Internet to research this topic if necessary.

Part V – Team Assessment (Team Requirement)

1. Rate each member of your team and yourself on the following points using the same 1 to 5 scale that you used in Part IV. Key the team member's name and the rating on each of the five following evaluation questions:
   a. Did the team member share good interview notes from his or her interview?
   b. Did the team member meet the timeline provided by your instructor?
   c. Did the team member participate effectively in the discussion?
   d. Did the team member respect the opinions of others and encourage all to share their thoughts?
   e. Did the team member do his or her fair share of the work?
2. For each team member, list the soft skills that were used most effectively during this activity.
3. In industry, leaders usually assess the results or outcomes produced by the whole team—not what each team member did. Would you be comfortable if the same standard were applied to your team— that is, the same grade would be given to all team members? Why or why not?

PREPARE FOR YOUR FUTURE

Skill Building

2d Improve Techniques

1. Key each line once.
2. Keep your eyes on the copy.

Reach with little finger; tap ENTER; *return to home key.*

15 if a lad;
16 is a sad fall
17 if a lass did ask
18 ask a lass; ask a lad
19 a;sldkfj a;sldkfj a;sldkfj
20 a; sl dk fj fj dk sl a; a;sldkfj
21 ik ik if if is is kid skid did lid aid laid said
22 ik kid ail die fie did lie ill ilk silk skill skid

2e Improve Keystroking

i

23 ik ik ik if is il ik id is if kid did lid aid ails
24 did lid aid; add a line; aid kids; ill kids; id is

n

25 nj nj nj an an and and end den ken in ink sin skin
26 jn din sand land nail sank and dank skin sans sink

e

27 el els elf elk lea lead fee feel sea seal ell jell
28 el eke ale jak lake elf els jaks kale eke els lake

2f Build Skill

29 dine in an inn; fake jade; lend fans; as sand sank
30 in nine inns; if an end; need an idea; seek a fee;
31 if a lad; a jail; is silk; is ill; a dais; did aid
32 adds a line; and safe; asks a lass; sail in a lake

2g Improve Techniques

Key each line once.

Keep your eyes on copy; key words at a steady pace.

33 send land skin faded sand kind line nine sale fail
34 dense sales lakes jaded likes jails salad kale inn
35 lad likes kale; lass likes silk; add a fee; is ill
36 kids in a lake; if in need; ask a lass; lad is ill

LESSON 2 E AND N   MODULE 1   1-8

Path to Workplace Success...Capstone Project

SOFT SKILLS INTERVIEW WITH FOLLOW-UP ACTIVITIES

This project can be completed by a team or by each student individually. The team approach is recommended.

1. Your instructor will determine whether this is a team (three or four members) or an individual activity and will provide a timeline for you to complete the activities.
2. Obtain contact information for team members if appropriate.

Part I – 15-Minute Face-to-Face Interview (Required of Each Student)

1. Each student must select an individual who hires, supervises, or manages employees in a career area of interest. The person may be in a company in which you or a family member is employed or someone from your neighborhood, your church, or another group with which you are affiliated.
2. Contact the individual and request an appointment for a face-to-face 15-minute interview. Explain that you are studying the importance of developing soft skills as part of your career preparation. Describe one or two soft skills you explored in this activity.
3. In a *Word* document, key the five questions in item 4 below, leaving space after each question to take brief notes on the answers.
4. Conduct the interview and take brief hand-written notes.
   a. What soft skills are your strengths that helped you most to get your job and progress in your career?
   b. What soft skills do the people you manage need most?
   c. When you are hiring, how do you determine if a candidate has the required soft skills?
   d. How do you help your employees improve their soft skills?
   e. What advice would you give me about developing good soft skills?

Part II – Edit and Share Notes (Required for Both Teams and Individuals)

1. Edit and key your notes using complete sentences.
2. Share your notes with each team member **or**, if you are working individually, share your notes with your instructor.

Part III – Selection of Five Most Important Soft Skills

Part III contains two options for students to determine what they believe are the five most important soft skills for workplace success based on interview data and their joint views or their individual views plus research data.

Option 1 is to be completed by students who are working in teams to make the decision.

Option 2 is to be completed by students who are working individually to make the decision.

PREPARE FOR YOUR FUTURE

Lesson 3 Review

Warmup Lesson 3a Warmup

```
home  1  ad ads lad fad dad as ask fa la lass jak jaks alas
   n  2  an fan and land fan flan sans sand sank flank dank
   i  3  is id ill dill if aid ail fail did kid ski lid ilk
  all 4  ade alas nine else fife ken; jell ink jak inns if;
```

Skill Building

3b Build Skill

Key each line once.

Lines 5–8: Think and key words. Make the space part of the word.

Lines 9–12: Think and key phrases. Do not key the vertical rules separating the phrases.

easy words
```
 5  if is as an ad el and did die eel fin fan elf lens
 6  as ask and id kid and ade aid eel feel ilk skis an
 7  ail fail aid did ken ale led an flan inn inns alas
 8  eel eke nee kneel did kids kale sees lake elf fled
```

easy phrases
```
 9  el el|id id|is is|eke eke|lee lee|ale ale|jill jak
10  is if|is a|is a|a disk|a disk|did ski|did ski|is a
11  sell a|sell a|sell a sled|fall fad|fall fad|fad is
12  sees a lake|sees a lake|as a deal|sell sled|a sale
```

3c Improve Keystroking

home row: fingers curved and upright
```
13  jak lad as lass dad sad lads fad fall la ask ad as
14  asks add jaks dads a lass ads flak adds sad as lad
```

upward reaches: straighten fingers slightly; return quickly to home position
```
15  fed die led ail kea lei did ale fife silk leak lie
16  sea lid deal sine desk lie ale like life idea jail
```

double letters: stroke double letters at a steady, unhurried pace
```
17  fee jell less add inn seek fall alee lass keel all
18  dill dell see fell eel less all add kiss seen sell
```

LESSON 3 REVIEW   MODULE 1   1-9

Path to Workplace Success...Develop Soft Skills

ACCOUNTABILITY

Accepting a position in the workplace indicates agreement and commitment to fulfilling the duties and responsibilities of the position and the expectations of the manager. The organization prospers when each team member consistently meets and exceeds the position's requirements and the expected goals. A few fundamental accountability practices are essential to be successful.

1. **Arrive on time.** Punctuality is an outward sign that the job is important to the employee, and arriving early to be ready to begin work at the starting time shows commitment to excellence.
2. **Stay on task.** With today's social media and cell phones, an employee is easily tempted to lose focus on tasks at hand to quickly check for messages or play a game. The expectation is for employees to complete work tasks on company time.
3. **Commit to quality work.** An excellent employee sets high standards beyond the minimum requirements and commits to excellence in all areas. Doing mediocre work is not an option.
4. **Hone organizational skills.** Prioritizing projects and meeting deadlines are critical to fulfilling job responsibilities. Acquiring organizational skills is essential.
5. **Devote time to professional development.** Growing in the job is also an outward sign of accountability. During performance review meetings, the employee and manager agree on areas of development that will assist the employee and the company.

For each of the scenarios below, you will complete an activity related to accountability. In a *Word* document, key a short explanation of what you have learned.

Scenario 1

Situation: You have a major report due in two weeks. Your team depends on your leadership and organizational skills to produce a quality product and to meet the deadline. You have a tendency to procrastinate.

Research: Locate at least four time management suggestions recommended by time management experts.

Apply: Select at least two strategies you will use to ensure this deadline is met with a quality product. What technology will you choose to assist you?

Write: Describe the two strategies you will use and identify the selected technology tool. Explain how these strategies will assist you in avoiding procrastination and meeting your deadline.

Scenario 2

Situation: Your manager is completing a task analysis for each employee to determine the needs of the organization. If you are a full-time student and not employed, keep the log for all your activities.

Research: Keep a log for one day (if you are a part-time employee, use the hours you work) and list all activities completed. Start at 8 a.m. and list every activity for each 30-minute increment until 5 p.m.

Apply: Analyze the log. Did you use time wisely? If not, how was time wasted? Could you rearrange work activities to achieve better results? Did you arrive on time? Did you begin work promptly?

Write: Describe at least two areas that you think were effective in your daily log. Explain at least two things you could have done differently that would have allowed you to be more productive.

3d Build Skill

19 and and land land el el elf elf self self ail nail
20 as as ask ask ad ad lad lad id id lid lid kid kids

phrases: think and key as phrases

21 if if|is is|jak jak|all all|did did|nan nan|elf elf
22 as a lad| ask dad| fed a jak| as all ask| sales fad
23 sell a lead|seal a deal|feel a leaf|if a jade sale
24 is a|is as if|a disk|aid all kids|did ski|is a silk

3e Improve Techniques

Key each line once.

Tap Space Bar with down-and-in motion.

reach review

25 ea sea lea seas deal leaf leak lead leas flea keas
26 as ask lass ease as asks ask ask sass as alas seas

27 sa sad sane sake sail sale sans safe sad said sand
28 le sled lead flee fled ale flea lei dale kale leaf

29 jn jn nj nj in fan fin an; din ink sin and inn an;
30 de den end fen an an and and ken knee nee dean dee

3f Timed Writing

Key lines 31–34 for 1'.
If you finish before time is up, repeat the lines.

Note:
1' = 1 minute
30" = 30 seconds

31 el eel eld elf sell self el dell fell elk els jell
32 in fin inn inks dine sink fine fins kind line lain
33 an and fan dean elan flan land lane lean sand sane
34 sell a lead; sell a jade; seal a deal; feel a leaf

LESSON 3 REVIEW   MODULE 1   1-10

Path to Workplace Success...Develop Soft Skills

COMMUNICATION—MAKING A FIRST IMPRESSION

Building a strong network of professionals is essential on the path to success. Presenting yourself in a confident and energetic manner forms a positive first impression that opens the door to professional friendships. These five tips are highly recommended by communication experts.

1. **Initiate a conversation.** It's hard to build a network without starting a conversation, and often you are the one who must initiate the conversation. It's okay if you are shy—get over it.
2. **Give a firm handshake.** Show your interest and enthusiasm by giving a firm handshake—touching web to web. Please look at the person while shaking hands, and do smile.
3. **Maintain direct eye contact.** Look at the person while talking and avoid the nervous tendency to look away. You do not want to give the impression you are nervous or bored.
4. **Present good posture.** Stand tall and do not slouch. Lean forward as you are talking to indicate interest in the other person.
5. **Dress appropriately**. Attention to one's dress conveys interest in the person you are meeting for perhaps the first time. This first impression can determine the potential impact you may have on that person.

For each of the scenarios below, you will practice one of these essential communication skills. In a *Word* document, key a short explanation of what you learned in the practice activity.

Scenario 1

Situation: You have just been hired in an entry-level position, and you begin work in one week. You understand how important making a positive impression is—especially on the first day on the job. A proper handshake is the first skill you have decided to practice.

Think/Discuss/Research: What are the characteristics of a proper handshake for making a positive and powerful first impression? What are some poor techniques?

Apply: Pair with someone and practice shaking hands. For comparison, discuss and practice both effective and ineffective techniques.

Write: Describe the characteristics of a powerful handshake that you have learned are important for the first day on the job and every day.

Scenario 2

Situation: You are doing well in your position, but you know today will be important as you are sharing an idea at a team meeting. You know you must project confidence and have effective eye contact while in conversation with the team members.

Think/Discuss/Research: Why is eye contact important when sharing your ideas with your team or supervisor? What impression are you making?

Apply: With a group of at least three people, share an idea that you have. Topics might include (1) a suggestion you have for an improvement in your community or school, (2) how a person's dress has impacted your first impression of that person, or (3) time management strategies that have helped you in the past. Or you can choose a topic with which you are comfortable. Your goal is to have eye contact with each person in the group by the conclusion of the conversation.

Write: Describe your experience. Did the topic make a difference in the quality of eye contact? Did you feel uncomfortable looking at your team while you talked? Did you receive any feedback from your team by looking at them? Did you feel nervous and feel the need to look away from your team? How can you improve your next conversation?

PREPARE FOR YOUR FUTURE

Lesson 4 Left Shift, H, T, Period

Warmup *Lesson 4a Warmup*

```
home row   1  al  as  ads  lad  dad  fad  jak  fall  lass  asks  fads  all;
   e/i/n   2  ed  ik  jn  in  knee  end  nine  line  sine  lien  dies  leis
all reaches 3 see a ski; add ink; fed a jak; is an inn; as a lad
     easy  4  an  dial  id  is  an  la  lake  did  el  ale  fake  is  land  a
```

New Keys

4b Left Shift and h

left shift Reach *down* with *left fourth* (little) finger; shift, tap, release.

h Reach to *left* with *right first* finger.

left shift

```
 5  J Ja Ja Jan Jan Jane Jana Ken Kass Lee Len Nan Ned
 6  and Ken and Lena and Jake and Lida and Nan and Ida
 7  Inn is; Jill Ina is; Nels is; Jen is; Ken Lin is a
```

h

```
 8  h hj hj he he she she hen aha ash had has hid shed
 9  h hj ha hie his half hand hike dash head sash shad
10  aha hi hash heal hill hind lash hash hake dish ash
```

4c All Reaches Learned

```
11  Nels Kane and Jake Jenn; she asked Hi and Ina Linn
12  Lend Lana and Jed a dish; I fed Lane and Jess Kane
13  I see Jake Kish and Lash Hess; Isla and Helen hike
```

4d Improve Keystroking

Key the drill once. Strive for good control.

```
14  he she held a lead; she sells jade; she has a sale
15  Ha Ja Ka La Ha Hal Ja Jake Ka Kahn La Ladd Ha Hall
16  Hal leads; Jeff led all fall; Hal has a safe lead
17  Hal Hall heads all sales; Jake Hess asks less fee;
```

Path to Workplace Success...Develop Soft Skills

CRITICAL THINKING AND DECISION MAKING

The ability to think critically helps you to make wise decisions that impact your work and your everyday life. Follow these five basic steps to make effective decisions.

1. **Identify the decision and collect facts**. Analyze objectively the situation requiring the decision. Get all the facts. Avoid making assumptions colored by stereotypes and preconceptions.
2. **Determine the options available**. Be creative in generating as many options as possible. In some cases options are predetermined.
3. **Analyze options carefully**. Try to view the situation from the perspective of everybody involved and that of the organization. Examine consequences for each person and for the organization.
4. **Select the best option and implement it**. Evaluate all of the options and get more facts if needed. Also consider what is necessary for the option to be successful. The way a decision is implemented often determines its success.
5. **Evaluate the effectiveness of the decision implemented**. Did it produce the desired results? Can it be improved?

For each of the scenarios below, key the following information in a *Word* document.

1. List the decision that must be made and the key facts to be considered. Add other things you think should be considered.
2. List the options available and the pros and cons of each.
3. Select the option and explain why it is best.

Scenario 1

Situation: Assume you live at home free and have saved enough money that you could (1) buy a small car so that you will have your own transportation, (2) use it to pay your tuition and other costs and avoid having to take out another substantial student loan, or (3) live in an apartment next year.

Facts: Family members lend you a car frequently when you need it. Most days you ride to classes with family or friends, but you would prefer to have your own car. Public transportation to your college is available and inexpensive. Your family provides free living and tries to help you, but they are not in a position to pay your tuition. You already have heavy student debt that you will have to begin paying as soon as you complete your program.

Decision: What decision is in your best interest? Why?

Scenario 2

Situation: You have been looking for a part-time job, and you have two opportunities: One is for the Foundation, which raises money for and supports your college. The other is a night job (6:00–11:00 p.m., four or five rotating nights a week) as the desk clerk at a local inn that is relatively inexpensive. With both jobs, you could work 20 to 30 hours per week. With the Foundation, you could work around your class schedule.

Facts: The Foundation duties include many that you are or will be studying—marketing, finance, accounting, management, and office technology. You would be able to interact with donors and board members who generally are business executives. The inn job duties include customer service skills, telephone skills, and basic office skills. The inn job pays $1 more per hour than the Foundation job. Before you make your decision, search for information about desk clerk jobs in hotels and inns and about jobs in educational-type foundations.

Decision: Which job would be in your best interest? Why? What other information do you need to make a good decision?

PREPARE FOR YOUR FUTURE

4e t and . (period)

t Reach *up* with *left first* finger.

t

18 t tf tf aft aft left fit fat fete tiff tie the tin
19 tf at at aft lit hit tide tilt tint sits skit this
20 hat kit let lit ate sit flat tilt thin tale tan at

Space once after a period.

. (period)

21 .l .l l.l fl. fl. L. L. Neal and J. N. List hiked.
22 Hand J. H. Kass a fan. Jeff did. Hank needs ideas.
23 Jane said she has a tan dish; Jed and Lee need it.

. (period) Reach *down* with *right third* finger.

4f Improve Keystroking

24 I did tell J. K. that Lt. Lee had left. He is ill.
25 tie tan kit sit fit hit hat; the jet left at nine.
26 I see Lila and Ilene at tea. Jane Kane ate at ten.
27 tf .l hj ft ki de jh tf ik ed hj de ft ki l. tf ik
28 elf eel left is sis fit till dens ink has delt ink
29 he he heed heed she she shelf shelf shed shed she
30 it is if id did lit tide tide tile tile list list

Skill Building

4g Build Skill

31 he has; he had; he led; he sleds; she fell; he is
32 it is; he hit it; he is ill; she is still; she is
33 Hal and Nel; Jade dishes; Kale has half; Jed hides
34 Hi Ken; Helen and Jen hike; Jan has a jade; Ken is

LESSON 4 LEFT SHIFT, H, T, PERIOD   MODULE I 1-12

Prepare for Your Future

Path to Workplace Success...Develop Critical Skills

SKILLS REQUIRED FOR CAREER SUCCESS

The skills required for specific jobs vary significantly depending on your field of interest, the organization that hires you, the type of job, and the level of the job. Regardless of these factors, a common base of knowledge and a common set of skills are required for virtually every job. These skills can be grouped into three categories:

- Technical skills
- Soft skills
- Conceptual skills

The earlier you start planning and preparing for your career, the more likely you are to be successful.

Technical Skills

These skills include:

- Knowledge
- Expertise
- Ability to do the job

Technical skills are especially important for entry-level positions. You will develop technical skills in the courses you take.

Examples of universal technical skills would be keyboarding skill and the ability to use applications such as *Word*, *Excel*, *Outlook*, and *PowerPoint*. The specific knowledge varies depending on the field, such as manager, medical professional, or architect.

Soft Skills

Soft skills are personal attributes, interpersonal skills, and emotional intelligence. Soft skills relate to the way you interact with other employees. Examples of soft skills that are required in most jobs include:

Softs skills are critical at every level. The remainder of this section focuses on soft skills.

- Communication skills
- Creativity
- Critical thinking and decision making
- Ethics, honesty, and integrity
- Accountability and responsibility
- Teamwork and collaboration
- Time management and productivity
- Work ethic

Conceptual Skills

Conceptual skills are the ability to see the big picture and how things fit together. Conceptual skills enable you to understand how your job fits into the overall business strategy of your organization.

You will learn conceptual skills in advanced courses and on the job. Conceptual skills are required for advancement in your position.

PREPARE FOR YOUR FUTURE

1a-27

Lesson 4R Review

Warmup *Lesson 4Ra Warmup*

home row	1	sad lad hall lad sale ask jak add aka fall fad ha;
review	2	H. Le Ki J. tan tin hit at tat nat hat nit Lt. hid
all reaches	3	Jed is in sales; Kate ate fish. Hank hit his head.
easy	4	sit dial and land fit then half din hand lend disk

Skill Building

4Rb Improve Keystroking

Key the drill once.

Think and key words and phrases.

words	5	slain tent Kent lent tea Jill Ned fed said laid he
phrases	6	he fakes	she hikes	his lead is safe	she and I fish
sentences	7	Nan is ill; He is at the lake; Jake is at the Inn.
sentences	8	Jed Hess did ski. Kit and I fished. Lisa ate fish.
sentences	9	Hank ate his salad. Jane has the disk in the tent.
sentences	10	He said that Nate left the lake and is at the Inn.

4Rc Build Skill

11 shelf lead jiff lead sand find dine kind fend tent
12 kale sake takes deal tended salad jaded dined left
13 if I sell it; seek a deal; find a tent; at the Inn
14 He asked Ken; I need a fan; He sells jade and land.
15 I like Hank and Jan; Leslie ate salad at the lake.

4Rd Timed Writing

1. Take two 1' timed writings. If you finish before time is up, begin again.
2. Use wordwrap.

Wordwrap: Text within a paragraph moves automatically from one line to the next; tap ENTER only to begin a new paragraph.

Use wordwrap

Janet sat in the tent; then she and I ate at the lake. Janet and her dad did find the disk in the tent at the lake. Helen and the dean ate a salad at the Inn; then she asked the dean if he had a keen idea. Jean said the dean had nine keen ideas.

Web-Based Computing 3 Social Media

SOCIAL MEDIA

Most people think of the first generation of the Internet as a vast online collection of information that can be accessed easily and at little or no cost. The role of the Internet user is simply to access information in a passive way for whatever purpose the user needs the information. As the Internet has matured, most people now think of it as an interactive tool that enables the user to contribute and collaborate with others. The role of the user is that of participant in an activity generally thought of as social networking.

SOCIAL MEDIA TOOLS

Many options exist that enable users to participate actively. The group of social media tools listed below is one way of looking at just a few of the different options available to users who want to participate actively.

Social networks are generally thought of as tools for sharing information with an online community of people with common interests. Facebook, LinkedIn, Twitter, and Google+ are examples of frequently used social networks.

Micro-blogging sites enable users to send brief messages (often 140 or fewer characters) to a group of people which in turn can be sent to other groups. Twitter and Tumblr are examples of micro-blogging sites.

Video sharing sites provide a platform for people to post videos to share with others. YouTube, Metacafe, Break, and Vimeo are examples of video-sharing sites.

Photo sharing sites provide a platform for people to post photographs to share with others. Examples include Flickr, Instagram, and Shutterfly.

Blogs are sites that provide publishing tools for people to post articles and various types of information to share with others and accept comments from readers. Examples of blog hosting sites include Blogger, WordPress, and Live Journal.

Bookmarking sites allow users to bookmark or tag sites that they recommend. Examples are Pinterest, Twitter, Reddit, and StumbleUpon.

DRILL 3

SOCIAL MEDIA

1. Search for one article in each of the categories using the name of the category shown in bold as the keywords. Use the article as the basis for deciding which site in that category you will visit.
2. In each category, visit the website of one of the examples of sites listed.
3. Select one site in any of the categories and contribute something to the site. Post a comment, photo, video, blog, or whatever you would like to post. You may have to register before posting to the site.

WEB-BASED COMPUTING: INTERNET, CLOUD, AND SOCIAL MEDIA

Lesson 5 R, Right Shift, C, O

Warmup *Lesson 5a Warmup*

home keys 1 a; ad add al all lad fad jak ask lass fall jak lad
t/h/i/n 2 the hit tin nit then this kith dint tine hint thin
left shift/. 3 I need ink. Li has an idea. Hank hit it. I see Kate.
all reaches 4 Jeff ate at ten; he left a salad dish in the sink.

New Keys

5b r and Right Shift

r Reach *up* with *left first* finger.

right shift Reach *down* with *right fourth* finger; shift, tap, release.

r

5 r rf rf riff riff fir fir rid ire jar air sir lair
6 rf rid ark ran rat are hare art rant tire dirt jar
7 rare dirk ajar lark rain kirk share hart rail tart

right shift

8 D D Dan Dan Dale Ti Sal Ted Ann Ed Alf Ada Sid Fan
9 and Sid and Dina and Allen and Eli and Dean and Ed
10 Ed Dana; Dee Falk; Tina Finn; Sal Alan; Anna Deeds

5c All Reaches Learned

11 Jane and Ann hiked in the sand; Asa set the tents.
12 a rake; a jar; a tree; a red fire; a fare; a rain;
13 Fred Derr and Rai Tira dined at the Tree Art Fair.

5d Improve Keystroking

Key each line once.

14 ir ir ire fir first air fair fire tire rid sir
15 fir jar tar fir flit rill till list stir dirt fire
16 Renee is ill. Fred read to her. Ed Finn left here.
17 All is still as Sarah and I fish here in the rain.
18 I still see a red ash tree that fell in the field.
19 Lana said she did sail her skiff in the dark lake.

LESSON 5 R, RIGHT SHIFT, C, O   MODULE I   1-14

4. Select Upload.

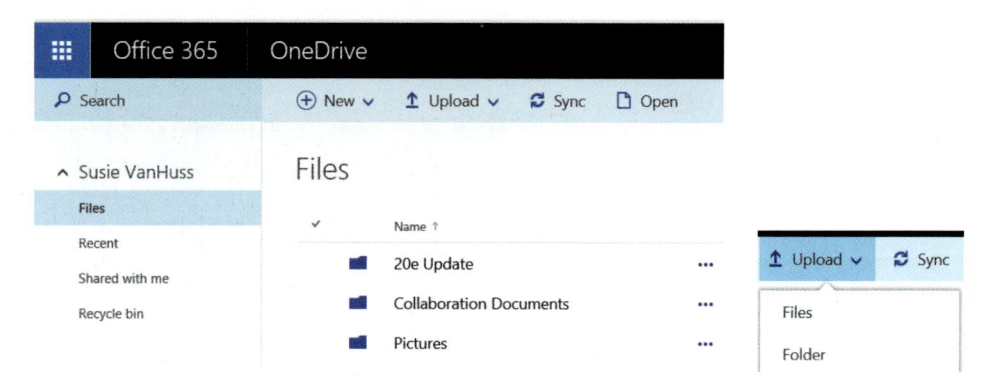

5. To add a file, click Upload and then select a document from your computer.
6. Select the desired file and it uploads. Double-click the file name to open and view it.

To create a document on your computer and save it to OneDrive:
1. Open Word and key the document.
2. On the File menu, click Save as.
3. Click your OneDrive and key the document name.
4. Click Save.

DRILL 2

wbc-onedrive

OneDrive

1. Access your OneDrive and upload the *wbc-onedrive* data file to your OneDrive.
2. Open it and review it.
3. Open a new Word document on your computer. Key and format the document shown at the right.
4. Save it to your OneDrive and close. (*my first onedrive document*)

My First OneDrive Document

Creating a Word document on my computer and saving it to my OneDrive is very easy to do. One of the advantages of saving the document on OneDrive is that I can access it from any location at any time. I can also share it with other members of my team.

Saving files on OneDrive will enable us to be more efficient with the team projects that we are currently trying to complete. Everybody will have access to the documents, and each team member can help with the editing.

WEB-BASED COMPUTING: INTERNET, CLOUD, AND SOCIAL MEDIA

5e c and o

c Reach *down* with *left second* finger.

o Reach *up* with *right third* finger.

c
20 c c cd cd cad cad can can tic ice sac cake cat sic
21 clad chic cite cheek clef sick lick kick dice rice
22 call acid hack jack lack lick cask crack clan cane

o
23 o ol ol old old of off odd ode or ore oar soar one
24 ol sol sold told dole do doe lo doll sol solo odor
25 onto door toil lotto soak fort hods foal roan load

Skill Building

5f Improve Keystroking

o/r
26 or or for for nor nor ore ore oar oar roe roe sore
27 a rose|her or|he or|he rode|or for|a door|her doll

e/n
28 en en end end ne ne need need ken ken kneel kneels
29 lend the|lend the|at the end|at the end|need their

c/o
30 ch ch check check ck ck hack lack jack co co cones
31 the cot|the cot|a dock|a dock|a jack|a jack|a cone

32 Carlo Rand can call Rocco; Cole can call Doc Cost.
all reaches 33 Trina can ask Dina if Nick Corl has left; Joe did.
34 Case sent Carole a nice skirt; it fits Lorna Rich.

5g Build Skill

i/t
35 is is tis tis it it fit fit tie tie this this lits
36 it is|it is|it is this|it is this|it sits|tie fits

37 Jack and Rona did frost nine of the cakes at last.
all reaches 38 Jo can ice her drink if Tess can find her a flask.
39 Ask Jean to call Fisk at noon; he needs her notes.

LESSON 5   R, RIGHT SHIFT, C, O

Web-Based Computing 2 Cloud Computing

CLOUD COMPUTING

Cloud computing is an evolving concept and, as such, is very difficult to define. Cloud computing can be simplified by examining the following concepts involved in cloud computing:

- A cloud computing system consists of many high-powered computer resources, such as servers, networks, storage applications, software applications, and information technology (IT) services, that can be easily accessed with a basic computer and an Internet connection.
- The resources can be accessed any time, from any location, and without any involvement of the organization providing the services. An example would be outlook.com or Gmail from Google. They are web-based, available on demand, and accomplished without interaction with the provider.
- The IT services provided to businesses are fee-based services. Some services may be provided free, such as *Google Docs* and *Office Online*. *Microsoft Office 365* is now offered on a subscription basis with special fees and, in some cases, free for education use.

WEB-BASED EMAIL

If you have a Gmail or an Outlook.com email address, you are currently using cloud computing. You may previously have had a Hotmail account. Microsoft has replaced it with free email from Outlook.com. You will need an Internet connection and a Microsoft account, such as an Outlook.com email account, to work with OneDrive in the next section. If you do not have one, use your browser to go to Outlook.com. Note the option to *Sign up now*. Click it and follow the instructions to establish your account.

OneDrive

You can get a free OneDrive account with your *Office 365 ProPlus* subscription or with *Windows 10*. If you do not have *Windows 10* or *Office 365 ProPlus*, you can get a free OneDrive account with your Outlook.com account. Follow the steps below to access OneDrive.

To access and add a document:
www.outlook.com

1. Sign in using your Outlook address or Microsoft ID and password.
2. Click the App Launcher at the left side of the blue bar.
3. Click OneDrive.

> **TIP**
>
> You can also access OneDrive from the Start menu. Tap the Windows key or click the Windows icon in the taskbar on the lower-left side of the screen to display the Start menu.

WEB-BASED COMPUTING: INTERNET, CLOUD, AND SOCIAL MEDIA

Lesson 5R Review

Warmup Lesson 5Ra Warmup

r/c/o/right shift 1 circle   order   record   Frank   Sarah   Tonia   Carlo   candor
r/c/o 2 effort   trick   scroll   control   clone   donor   salon   corn
right shift 3 Sandra   Forde   Addie   Crone   Stan   Allison   Rhonda   candor
all reaches 4 Jeff   drank   his   cold   tea   and   ate   cookies   in   a   tent.

Skill Building

Think and key words and phrases as units.

5Rb Improve Keystroking

1. Key each line once.
2. Keep your eyes on the copy.

words
5 choice   rejoice   north   crank   drank   cross   craft   order
6 creaked   kitchen   store   lost   frost   train   rained   horn

phrases
7 to the east | I left at noon | reach it | he liked Janet
8 Fred chose one | Connie cooked | Daniel ate fried food

sentences
9 Carl and Jack left for a short train ride at noon.
10 Lee and Jo can cook for their friends in the tent.

5Rc Build Skill

o/r
11 or cork for nor sore tore rote lore snore ore core
12 his or her | she rode | at the door | she tore her skirt

c/o
13 close choose color cork corn coal ocean cold scorn
14 close the door | choose a color | for a dock | cook corn

all reaches
15 Joan and Clark selected a nice color for the dock.
16 Dick sent Lori a nice skirt and Frank a red shirt.

5Rd Timed Writing

1. Key a 1' timing; use wordwrap—do not return at the end of the line. If you finish before time is up, begin again.
2. Key a 1' timed writing at a slower but fluent pace.

wordwrap ↓

Connie said that her son can cook for her friends at noon. He is a trained chef and likes to cook for others. He can locate and choose the food. Harold offered to do all of the dishes. I think that is also a nice offer.

Web-Based Computing: Internet, Cloud, and Social Media

Web-Based Computing 1 Internet

OVERVIEW OF WEB-BASED COMPUTING

Three key components of web-based computing—the Internet, cloud computing, and social media—are covered in this section. These topics are overlapping and have many common advantages and disadvantages, but looking at them separately makes it easier to understand the concepts and to apply them in a useful manner.

INTERNET

> **TIP**
>
> Read the *Digital Citizenship* article in Level 1b, pages 113–114 to learn more about using the Internet effectively and safely.

Most students have had significant experience surfing the web. If you haven't, a quick terminology review might be helpful.

Internet A global collection of interconnected networks used to share information. To access the Internet, you must have an Internet connection and a browser.

Browser A software program installed on your computer, such as *Internet Explorer*, *Edge*, *Chrome*, or *Firefox*, that enables you to access web pages.

URL A **U**niform **R**esource **L**ocater is a unique web address for each web page. Clicking the URL http://www.cengage.com will enable you to log in if you have an account and to create an account if you do not have one. The protocol is **http://**, the location is **www** (World Wide Web), and the domain is **com** (commercial). Each segment of the address is separated by a period.

Search Engine A website, such as *Bing*, *Google*, or *Yahoo!*, that enables you to locate specific information efficiently on the web by using keywords that describe the topic.

Bookmark A bookmark is a saved URL that you can access quickly by adding it to a **Favorites List**. To visit the website again, click Favorites and select it.

DRILL 1

WEB ACTIVITIES

1. Launch *Internet Explorer* or the browser on your computer.

2. Key the URL **http://www.cengage.com** in the address box at the top of the page. Search for *Keyboarding Course Lessons 1–25*. View the information available.

3. Click the View favorites, feeds, and history button on the menu bar and select Add to Favorites. Click the Add button.

4. Click the Back arrow at the top of your browser twice to return to the opening page. Then key **weather**, your city, and your state and click the Search Web button. Check your weather today.

Lesson 6 W, Comma, B, P

Warmup *Lesson 6a Warmup*

home row 1 ask a lad; a fall fad; had a salad; ask a sad jak;
o/t 2 to do it; to toil; as a tot; do a lot; he told her
c/r 3 cots are; has rocks; roll cot; is rich; has an arc
all reaches 4 Holt can see Dane at ten; Jill sees Frank at nine.

New Keys

6b w and , (comma)

w Reach *up* with *left third* finger.

, (comma) Reach *down* with *right second* finger.

w

5 w ws ws was was wan wit low win jaw wilt wink wolf
6 sw sw w sow ow now now row row own own wow wow owe
7 to sew; to own; was rich; was in; is how; will now

, (comma)

8 k, k, k, irk, ilk, ask, oak, ark, lark, jak, rock,
9 skis, a dock, a fork, a lock, a fee, a tie, a fan,
10 Joe, Ed, and I saw Nan, Ann, and Wes in a new car.

6c All Reaches Learned

11 Win, Lew, Drew, and Walt will walk to West Willow.
12 Ask Ho, Al, and Jared to read the code; it is new.
13 The window, we think, was closed; we felt no wind.

6d Improve Techniques

Key each line once.

Good posture builds an attitude of preciseness.

14 walk wide sown wild town went jowl wait white down
15 a dock, a kit, a wick, a lock, a row, a cow, a fee
16 Joe lost to Ron; Fiji lost to Cara; Don lost to Al
17 Kane will win; Nan will win; Rio will win; Di wins
18 Walter is in Reno; Tia is in Tahoe; then to Hawaii

LESSON 6 W, COMMA, B, P MODULE 1 1-17

DRILL 23

COMPOSE PARAGRAPHS ABOUT CLOUD COMPUTING

1. Review the "Composition" section of Appendix C.
2. Read information about the topic cloud computing from a variety of sources. Ideas for locating articles are listed below.
   a. *Web-Based Computing—Cloud Computing* section on pages 103–104.
   b. If you have access to the Internet, key the keyword phrase **cloud computing** and browse for pertinent information.
3. Summarize the information you read about cloud computing in your own words. Compose at least two paragraphs; double-space using the following as a suggested outline.
   a. Explain what cloud computing is and how it is used for communication.
   b. Describe some of the advantages of using cloud computing and some of the disadvantages.
4. Edit and proofread the paragraphs carefully.
5. Save and close. (*com-drill23*)

DRILL 24

COMPOSE PARAGRAPHS ABOUT SOCIAL MEDIA

1. Review the "Composition" section of Appendix C.
2. Read information about social media and the variety of applications available to users today. Ideas for locating articles are listed below.
   a. *Web-Based Computing—Social Media* section on page 105.
   b. If you have access to the Internet, browse for pertinent information about social media tools. You may prefer to research one of the social media tools referenced in the article on page 105.
3. Summarize the information you read about social media applications in your own words. Compose at least two paragraphs; double-space using the following as a suggested outline.
   a. Explain what is and how social media tools are used for communication.
   b. Describe some of the advantages of using social media tools and some of the disadvantages.
4. Edit and proofread the paragraphs carefully.
5. Save and close. (*com-drill24*)

COMMUNICATION SKILLS

6e b and p

b Reach *down* with *left first* finger.

p Reach *up* with *right fourth* (little) finger.

b

19 bf bf bf biff fib fib bib bib boa boa fib fibs rob
20 bf bf bf ban ban bon bon bow bow be be rib rib sob
21 a dob, a cob, a crib, a lab, a slab, a bid, a bath

p

22 p; p; pa pa; pal pal pan pan pad par pen pep paper
23 pa pa; lap lap; nap nap; hep ape spa asp leap clap
24 a park, a pan, a pal, a pad, apt to pop, a pair of

Skill Building

6f Improve Keystroking

all reaches learned
25 Barb and Bob wrapped a pepper in paper and ribbon.
26 Rip, Joann, and Dick were all closer to the flash.
27 Bo will be pleased to see Japan; he works in Oslo.

reach review
28 ki kid did aid lie hj has has had sw saw wits will
29 de dell led sled jn an en end ant hand k, end, kin

s/w
30 ws ws lows now we shown win cow wow wire jowl when
31 Wes saw an owl in the willow tree in the old lane.

b/p
32 bf bf fib rob bid ;p p; pal pen pot nap hop cap bp
33 Rob has both pans in a bin at the back of the pen.

6g Build Skill

34 to do|can do|to bow|ask her|to nap|to work|is born
35 for this|if she|is now|did all|to see|or not|or if

all reaches
36 Dick owns a dock at this lake; he paid Ken for it.
37 Jane also kept a pair of owls, a hen, and a snake.

38 Blair soaks a bit of the corn, as he did in Japan.
39 I blend the cocoa in the bowl when I work for Leo.

LESSON 6 W, COMMA, B, P

DRILL 20

COMPOSE PARAGRAPHS

1. Review the "Composition" section of Appendix C.
2. Write a paragraph of three to five sentences about each of the five topics.
3. Edit and proofread each paragraph carefully.
4. Save and close. (*com-drill20*)

1. Write a paragraph introducing yourself to your instructor. Describe the things you think are important in helping her or him get to know you better.
2. Write a paragraph describing one or more of your hobbies.
3. A relative gave you $500 today and suggested that you use it wisely. Write a paragraph discussing what you would do with the money and why you made that decision.
4. You have decided to become more physically fit. Therefore, you plan to improve your eating habits and become more physically active. Write a paragraph describing how you plan to achieve your goal.
5. Two summer jobs are available at a local recreational center. One job is for an assistant in the administrative office; the other is for an assistant to the recreation director.

    The job in the administrative office is varied and includes answering the telephone, scheduling appointments, working with visitors who come to the office, keeping basic records, and doing general office work.

    The job working with the recreation director is an outdoor job that involves coordinating activities for children in various sports, helping to teach children the sports and how to play together and helping to maintain the various venues.

    Write a paragraph describing the job you would prefer and why you made that selection. Explain how you would be good for the job and how it would be good for you.

DRILL 21

COMPOSE AN EMAIL

1. Review the "Composition" section of Appendix C.
2. Compose an email to your instructor following the instructions.
3. Edit and proofread your email very carefully.
4. Save and close. (*com-drill21*)

Describe the job that you selected in Drill 20 and why you chose it. Ask your instructor about the possibility of meeting with you at his or her convenience to help you prepare for your interview. Also ask if you may use her or his name as a reference.

DRILL 22

COMPOSE FOLLOW-UP EMAIL

1. Review the "Composition" section of Appendix C.
2. Compose an email that is a follow-up to the one you prepared in Drill 21. See specific instructions at the right.
3. Edit and proofread your email very carefully.
4. Save and close. (*com-drill22*)

Your instructor met with you and gave you many helpful suggestions about preparing for the interview. These suggestions included visiting the recreational center website and learning about the center prior to the interview, tips on dress and conduct during the interview, tips on the kinds of questions that are normally asked during interviews, and overall ways to present yourself more effectively. Your instructor agreed to serve as a reference for you.

Thank your instructor for taking the time to meet with you and indicate how much you appreciate the tips for interviewing that were provided. Be specific enough to show that you listened carefully and learned from the counseling session. Also thank your instructor for being willing to serve as a reference.

COMMUNICATION SKILLS

Lesson 7 Review

Warmup *Lesson 7a Warmup*

all 1 We often can take the older jet to Paris and back.
home 2 a; sl dk fj a;sl dkfj ad as all ask fads adds asks
1st row 3 Ann Bascan and Cabal Naban nabbed a cab in Canada.
3rd row 4 Rip went to a water show with either Pippa or Pia.

7b Improve Keystroking

5 ad la as in if it lo no of oh he or so ok pi be we
6 an ace ads ale aha a fit oil a jak nor a bit a pew
7 ice ades born is fake to jail than it and the cows
8 Ask Jed. Dr. Hand left at ten; Dr. Crowe, at nine.

Skill Building

7c Improve Techniques
Key each line once.

Keep your eyes on the textbook copy as you key.

9 ws ws was was wan wan wit wit pew paw nap pop bawl
10 bf bf fb fb fob fob rib rib be be job job bat back
11 p; p; asp asp pan pan ap ap ca cap pa nap pop prow
12 Barb and Bret took an old black robe and the boot.
13 Walt saw a wisp of white water renew ripe peppers.
14 Pat picked a black pepper for the picnic at Parks.

7d Build Skill

15 Jake held a bit of cocoa and an apricot for Diane.
16 Dick and I fish for cod on the docks at Fish Lake.
17 Kent still held the dish and the cork in his hand.
18 As far as I know, he did not read all of the book.

DRILL 18

PROOFREADING

1. Review the "Proofreading" section of Appendix C.
2. Key the document double-spaced, correcting errors as you key. *Hint:* Ten errors are planted in the two paragraphs.
3. Follow the proofreading and editing procedures in the previous drill.
4. Save and close. (com-drill18)

Email, once considered to be the most frequently used an misused means of communication is being surpassed by instant messaging and social networking applications, such as Facebook, Instagram, Pinterest, and Twitter. Blogs and wikis also accounts for many messages send today.

Taking advantage of these highly collaborative and targeted means of communication, businesses are creating their own social networking and micro-blogging sites. How ever, business executives share the following concerns: some lack of security for company information, the ease with which messages can be received by unintended recepients, communications being to causal, poor quality of messages, and inappropriateness of the medium for certain types of messages. To be a successful business communicator each employe must understand company communication policy and adhere to the established procedures and practices.

Composition

DRILL 19

COMPOSE SENTENCES

1. Review the "Composition" section of Appendix C.
2. Write and edit one to three complete sentences about each to answer the five questions.
3. Key the response to the question and tap ENTER twice between questions. Try to use an active, direct style of writing when possible.
4. Save and close. (*com-drill19*)

Example
Passive: I find baseball to be enjoyable, and I played well enough to be given the opportunity to play on the team.
Active: I enjoy playing baseball and earned a spot on the team.

1. Where do you live (street name, city or town, and state), and what do you like most and least about the place where you live?
2. Where do you attend school, and what do you like most and least about it?
3. What is your favorite subject, and why do you like it?
4. What is your least favorite subject, and why is it the least favorite?
5. How do you generally spend your time that is not spent in school or sleeping?

7e Textbook Keying

Key each line once.

Words: key as single unit; phrases: say and key fluently; sentences: work for fluency.

words 19 a an pan so sot la lap ah own do doe el elf to tot
phrases 20 if it | to do | it is | do so | for the | he works | if he bid
sentences 21 Jess ate all of the peas in the salad in the bowl.

words 22 bow bowl pin pint for fork forks hen hens jak jaks
phrases 23 is for | did it | is the | we did a | and so | to see | or not
sentences 24 I hid the ace in a jar as a joke; I do not see it.

words 25 chap chaps flak flake flakes prow prowl work works
phrases 26 as for the | as for the | and to the | to see it | and did
sentences 27 As far as I know, he did not read all of the book.

7f Timed Writing

1. Take two 1' timed writings. If you finish before time is up, begin again.
2. Use wordwrap; do not tap ENTER at the ends of the lines.

Goal: 12 gwam

wordwrap ↓

gwam 1'

It is hard to fake a confident spirit. We will do   10
better work if we approach and finish a job and   19
know that we will do the best work we can and then   29
not fret.   31

| 1 | 2 | 3 | 4 | 5 | 6 | 7 | 8 | 9 | 10 |

7g Build Speed

STANDARD PLAN — For Building Speed

You can build speed by practicing diligently and purposefully.

1. Focus on short timings and gradually increase the length.
2. Ignore errors.
3. Key the line first striving for fluency; do not time.
4. Take short timings (30") and gradually increase the length.
5. Strive to increase speed on each timing.

1. Key each line once for fluency.
2. Take two 30" writings on each line. Do not save the timings.

Goal: Reach the end of the line before time is up.

28 Dan took her to the show.
29 Jan lent the bowl to the pros.
30 Hold the wrists low for this drill.
31 Jessie fit the black panel to the shelf.
32 Patrick cooked breakfast for Jill and her friends.

LESSON 7 REVIEW

DRILL 16

PROOFREADING

1. Review the "Proofreading" section of Appendix C.
2. Proofread each sentence and then key the sentence, correcting the error in it.
3. Proofread again to ensure that you did not make any other keying errors. Correct any errors you find.
4. Save and close. (com-drill16)

1. The only way to proofread numbers effectively is too compare the keyed copy to the original source.
2. Concentration is an important proofreading skill, especially it you proofread on screen.
3. May people skip over the small words when they proofread; yet the small words often contain errors.
4. They sole 15 baskets at $30 each for a total of $450. Always check the math when you proofread.
5. Names are often spelled in different ways; there fore, you must verify the spelling to ensure that you use the correct version.
6. Reading copy on a word-bye-word basis is necessary to locate all errors.
7. Checking for words that may have been left is also important.
8. Of course, you should also check to make sure the content in correct.
9. Check dates carefully, such as the Fourth of July holiday is celebrated on July 3.
10. Check that details are accurate, such as found in the following sentence: After much discussion, the couple agreed to have their wedding at six o'clock in the morning.
11. Check that each pronoun matches their antecedent in number.
12. You want to verify that the subject and verb agrees in each sentence.
13. Always remember to not split an infinitive.
14. Students must realize that spell check does not mark all there spelling and typographical errors.
15. Knowing the document was error free, satisfaction was felt by Daniel.

DRILL 17

PROOFREADING

1. Review the "Proofreading" section of Appendix C.
2. Key the paragraph, correcting errors as you key. *Hint:* Ten errors are planted in the paragraph.
3. Follow the proofreading and editing procedures in the previous drill.
4. Save and close. (com-drill17)

The 1st quarter revenue figures for region IV was released today and you will be pleased to learn that once again the team exceded it's first quarter revenue budget. Congradulations! All member of the team exceeded their budget for the first quarter. We have consistently met both team goals for the passed 3 years; but rarely has every member of the team exceeded the budget plan.

COMMUNICATION SKILLS

Lesson 8 G, Question Mark, X, U

Warmup Lesson 8a Warmup

```
 all  1  Dick will see Job at nine if Rach sees Pat at one.
 w/b  2  As the wind blew, Bob Webber saw the window break.
 p/,  3  Pat, Pippa, or Cap has prepared the proper papers.
 all  4  Bo, Jose, and Will fed Lin; Jack had not paid her.
```

New Keys

8b g and ? (question mark)

g Reach to *right* with *left first* finger.

? Left SHIFT; reach *down* with *right fourth* finger.

Question mark: The question mark is followed by one space.

```
        g
    5   g g gf gaff gag grog fog frog drag cog dig fig gig
    6   gf go gall flag gels slag gala gale glad glee gals
    7   golf flog gorge glen high logs gore ogle page grow

        ? (question mark)
    8   ? ?; ?; ? ? Who?   When?  Where?  Who is?  Who was she?
    9   Who is here? Was it she? Was it he? Did Pablos go?
   10   Did Geena? Did he? What is that? Was Joe here too?
```

8c All Reaches Learned

```
   11  Has Ginger lost her job? Were her last bills here?
   12  Phil did not want the boats to get here this soon.
   13  Loris Shin has been ill; Frank, a doctor, saw her.
```

8d Improve Keystroking

1. Key each line once.
2. Keep your eyes on the textbook copy.

```
reach   14  ws ws hj hj tf tf ol ol rf rf ed ed cd cd bf bf p;
review  15  wed bid has old hold rid heed heed car bed pot pot

        16  gf gf gin gin rig ring go gone no nog sign got dog
  g     17  to go|to go|go on|go in|go in|to go in|in the sign

        18  ?; ?;? who? when? where? how? what? who? It is he?
  ?     19  Is she? Is he? Did I lose Paul? Is Gabe all right?
```

DRILL 14

PROOFREADING

1. Review the "Proofreading" section of Appendix C.
2. Key the paragraph, correcting errors as you key. *Hint:* Ten errors are planted in the paragraph.
3. Follow the proofreading and editing procedures in the previous drill.
4. Save and close. (com-drill14)

Editing and proof-reading is just as important for internal documents as for external documents. However, many people wrong beleive that external documents need carefully scrutiny but documents that stay with in the company do not matter as much. If your emails are memos frequently contain errors, fellow workers and supervisors may think that you are careless or have poor communication skills. This perception may harm your chances for advancement within you company. Developing good communication skills, and applying those skills to each document that you produce will enhance your career opportunities.

DRILL 15

PROOFREADING

1. Review the "Proofreading" section of Appendix C.
2. Key the paragraph, correcting errors as you key. *Hint:* Ten errors are planted in the paragraph.
3. Follow the proofreading and editing procedures in the previous drill.
4. Save and close. (com-drill15)

Blogs are web logs (personnel journals) that is typically owned and maintained by 1 person. A blog gives it's owner a place to write about any topic of interest. It is typical updated frequently, much as a travelog or dairy would be. Only the owner can edit, delete, or add to the content of a blog. Visitors can comment about the content but they cannot change if. Wikis differ from blogs in this respect, since any body can change anything in a wiki.

COMMUNICATION SKILLS

New Keys

8e x and u

x Reach *down* with *left third* finger.

u Reach *up* with *right first* finger.

Concentrate on correct reaches.

x

20 x x xs xs ox ox lox sox fox box ex hex lax hex fax
21 sx six sax sox ax fix cox wax hex box pox sex text
22 flax next flex axel pixel exit oxen taxi axis next

u

23 u uj uj jug jut just dust dud due sue use due duel
24 uj us cud but bun out sun nut gun hut hue put fuel
25 dual laud dusk suds fuss full tuna tutus duds full

Skill Building

8f Improve Keystroking

Think and key phrases.

26 Paige Power liked the book; Josh can read it next.
27 Next we picked a bag for Jan; then she, Jan, left.
28 Is her June account due? Has Jo ruined her credit?
29 nut cue hut sun rug us six cut dug axe rag fox run
30 out of the sun|cut the action|a fox den|fun at six
31 That car is not junk; it can run in the next race.

8g Timed Writing

1. Take two 1' timed writings. If you finish before time is up, begin again. (The dot above various words equals 2 *gwam*; each number is another 4 *gwam*.)
2. Use wordwrap; do not tap ENTER at the end of lines.

Goal: 14 *gwam*

wordwrap

How a finished job will look often depends on how we feel about our work as we do it. Attitude has a definite effect on the end result of work we do.
Tap ENTER once
When we are eager to begin a job, we relax and do better work than if we start the job with an idea that there is just nothing we can do to escape it.

LESSON 8   G, QUESTION MARK, X, U

Proofreading

DRILL 12

PROOFREADERS' MARKS

1. Review the "Proofreading" section of Appendix C.
2. Key the paragraph, correcting errors as you key. Refer to the proofreaders' marks in Appendix C.
3. Proofread the copy carefully on the screen following the proofreading guides in Appendix C. Make appropriate corrections including your keying errors.
4. Preview the document and print it.
5. Proofread the hard copy carefully and mark any uncorrected errors using proofreaders' marks. Make the corrections in the document file.
6. Save and close. (*com-drill12*)

Instant messaging (IM) began as a popular tool for determining if friends were on line and were willing to play games or chat. Now its moved to the corporate setting. The number of instant messages send at work increased 110% last year. with IM, messages fly back and forth, faster then email. Workers use IM to get urgently needed information, send important news signal that a client is waiting, and avoid telephone tag. 2 problems with instant messaging have been lack of security an the inability to keep a record of Correspondence. New business versions of Im software have addressed these issues.

DRILL 13

PROOFREADING

1. Review the "Proofreading" section of Appendix C.
2. Key the paragraph, correcting errors as you key. *Hint:* Ten errors are planted in the paragraph.
3. Proofread the copy carefully on the screen. Make needed corrections. Preview the document and print it.
4. Proofread the hard copy carefully and mark any uncorrected errors, using proofreaders' marks.
5. Make the corrections in the document file.
6. Save and close. (*com-drill13*)

The executive committee plans to meet on April second at one o'clock in room 201 to develop a strategic plan to market our new products At it's last monthly meeting David Westfield, a leading Consultant with the Jones Group presented several alternatives. Mr Westfield will present a proposal at this meeting for consulting services from the Jones Group to assist us in planning the new product launch.

COMMUNICATION SKILLS

1a-17

Lesson 8R Review

Warmup *Lesson 8Ra Warmup*

reach review 1 Jack is glad about the response to the fundraiser.
p 2 The local paper printed their public opinion poll.
b 3 Four babies babbled as big bears rode brown bikes.
easy 4 The newest prices were not shown to her and to me.

Skill Building

Move fingers up and down without moving your hands.

8Rb Improve Techniques

1. Key each line once.
2. Keep your eyes on the copy.

home row 5 add hash shall slash salads flags alfalfa fall ask
6 A fresh salad dish was added for staff and guests.
third row 7 tire wrote rewrite ripe proper papers trip picture
8 A reporter edited the newspaper stories with ease.
1st/2nd fingers 9 returned guest changes kicked tonight flight drink
10 Ed kept doing kind deeds for the children in need.

8Rc Timed Writing

1. Take two 1' timed writings. If you finish before time is up, begin again.
2. Use wordwrap; do not tap ENTER at the ends of the lines.

gwam 1'

Luck looks at those who are prepared for it. Think   10
about what is needed to be where one should be in a   21
decade. What will it take? Will it take additional   31
education or perhaps just other experience? One sets   41
a large goal and then works through a series of other   52
lesser goals to get there. One needs to be able to   62
know what success looks like as one finishes one of   73
the goals to get to the next one. If one does it   83
well, people will think it was all luck.   91

| 1 | 2 | 3 | 4 | 5 | 6 | 7 | 8 | 9 | 10 |

8Rd Build Speed

Key two 30" timings on each line. Try to increase your speed the second time.

We use the web and work online.
We shop online and use social networks.
The web helps us as we work and share data.
While working online, we need to keep our data safe.

Spelling

DRILL 10

SPELLING

1. Review the "Spelling Rules" section of Appendix C.
2. Proofread the sentences. If the word shown in bold is spelled correctly, key **Yes**. If the work is misspelled, key **No**.
3. Save and close. (*com-drill10*)

1. The sign in the store window stated that **turkeyes** are in the meat department.
2. Only cash or **checkes** are accepted in the new ice cream shop.
3. The postal clerk checked the **weight** of the package.
4. Students with fewer than three absences **recieved** special recognition.
5. Two **keys** were issued to each residence hall student.
6. How can celebrity chefs measure **accurately** without using a measuring spoon?
7. The complimentary closing very **truley** yours is seldom used in business correspondence.
8. You will find a list of school **supplies** in a display at the front of the store.
9. Be sure you have **submited** your travel budget request by the first of the year.
10. My parents traveled to Vermont for the turning of the **leaves**.
11. The rancher was happy to report the safe birth of two **calfs** this morning.
12. Until the attendant announced that electronic devices could be used on the aircraft, the **children** were bored.
13. The babysitter cooked roast and **potatos** for the little boy.
14. The roller coast ride was **exciteing** to all the family members.
15. **Flys** are attracted by uncovered food left on the picnic table.

DRILL 11

COMPREHENSIVE REVIEW

1. Key the paragraph, correcting errors as you key. The 15 errors include capitalization, number expression, subject-verb agreement, pronoun case and agreement, commas, and spelling errors.
2. Proofread and correct errors.
3. Save and close. (*com-drill11*)

    Scheduled for Monday june 15th at one p.m. in room two this week's orientation training session focuses on netiquette. in preparation for this meeting each participant are asked to bring thier three pet peeves regarding misuse of email instant messaging and discussion forumes. Prizes will be awarded to the first 5 individuals whom register.

COMMUNICATION SKILLS

Lesson 9 Q, M, V, Apostrophe

Warmup Lesson 9a Warmup

all letters 1 Lex gripes about cold weather; Fred is not joking.
space bar 2 Is it Di, Jo, or Al? Ask Lt. Coe, Bill; She knows.
easy 3 We did rush a bushel of cut corn to the six ducks.
easy 4 He is to go to the Tudor Isle of England on a bus.

New Keys

9b q and m

q Reach *up* with *left fourth* finger.

m Reach *down* with *right first* finger.

q

5 q qa qa quad quad quaff quant queen quo quit quick
6 qa qu qa quo quit quod quid quip quads quote quiet
7 quite quilts quart quill quakes quail quack quaint

m

8 m mj mj jam man malt mar max maw me mew men hem me
9 m mj ma am make male mane melt meat mist amen lame
10 malt meld hemp mimic tomb foam rams mama mire mind

9c All Reaches Learned

11 Quin had some quiet qualms about taming a macaque.
12 Jake Coxe had questions about a new floor program.
13 Max was quick to join the big reception for Lidia.

9d Improve Keystroking

1. Key each line once; keep your elbows at your side.
2. Keep your eyes on the textbook copy.

m/x
14 me men ma am jam am lax, mix jam; the hem, six men
15 Emma Max expressed an aim to make a mammoth model.

q/u
16 qa qu aqua aqua quit quit quip quite pro quo squad
17 Did Quin make a quick request to take the Qu exam?

g/n
18 fg gn gun gun dig dig nag snag snag sign grab grab
19 Georgia hung a sign in front of the union for Gib.

Subject-Verb Agreement

DRILL 8

SUBJECT-VERB AGREEMENT

1. Review the "Subject/Verb Agreement" section of Appendix C.
2. Key the sentences, choosing the correct verb.
3. Proofread and correct errors.
4. Save and close. (*com-drill8*)

1. Everything in the packages (is/are) securely wrapped.
2. None of the mountains (is/are) visible today.
3. Many of the drivers (is/are) following too closely.
4. Everyone (is/are) expected to attend the seminar.
5. All of the candidates (was/were) invited to the debate.
6. Nobody (want/wants) to be left behind.
7. Few of the animals (is/are) outside today.
8. Each of the puppies (is/are) given a new collar upon adoption.
9. Half of the adoptions (is/are) dogs fewer than six months of age.
10. A number of the animal adoptions (is/are) to senior citizens.

DRILL 9

SUBJECT-VERB AGREEMENT

1. Review the "Subject/Verb Agreement" section of Appendix C.
2. Key the sentences, choosing the correct verb and applying the correct commas and capitalization.
3. Proofread and correct errors.
4. Save and close. (*com-drill9*)

1. both of the curies (was/were) nobel prize winners.
2. mr. and mrs. thomas funderburk, jr. (was/were) married on Saturday november 23 1936 and they established their first home in Seattle Washington.
3. my sister and her college roommates (plan/plans) to tour london paris and rome this summer.
4. Emma Greer our new information manager (suggest/suggests) the following salutation when using an attention line: ladies and gentlemen.
5. the body language expert (place/places) his hand on his cheek as he says "touch your hand to your chin."
6. the japanese child (enjoy/enjoys) the american food her hosts (serve/serves) her.
7. the final exam (cover/covers) chapters 1-5.
8. Each of the directors in the sales department (has/have) given (his or her, their) approval.
9. According to bylaw 5-21 all of the candidates (are/is) invited to the debate at boston college.
10. Neither Jill nor her parents (expect/expects) to arrive at their destination before midnight.
11. Either Rebecca or Leah (buy/buys) groceries on saturday morning but they both (do/does) laundry on thursday night.
12. The total cost of the trip to las vegas (is/are) $2,525.25.

COMMUNICATION SKILLS

9e v and ' (apostrophe)

v Reach *down* with *left first* finger.

' Reach to the *right* with the *right fourth* finger.

Apostrophe: The apostrophe shows either omission (as Rob't for Robert or it's for it is) or possession when used with nouns (as Joe's hat).

v

20 v vf vf vie vie via via vim vat vow vile vale vote
21 vf vf ave vet ova eve vie dive five live have lave
22 cove dove over aver vivas hive volt five java jive

' (apostrophe)

23 '; '; it's it's Rod's; it's Bo's hat; we'll do it.
24 We don't know if it's Lee's pen or Norma's pencil.
25 It's ten o'clock; I won't tell him that he's late.

Skill Building

9f Improve Keystroking

26 It's Viv's turn to drive Iva's van to Ava's house.
v/? 27 Qua, not Vi, took the jet; so did Owen. Didn't he?
28 Wasn't Vada Baxter a judge at the post garden show?
29 Viola said she has moved six times in five months.
30 Does Dave live on Vines Avenue? Must he leave now?
q/? 31 Did Viv vote? Can Paque move it? Did Valerie quit?
32 Didn't Raquel quit Carl Quent after their quarrel?

9g Timed Writing

Take a 1' timing on each paragraph. If you finish before time is up, start the paragraph again. The dots equal 2 words. Use wordwrap.

wordwrap

The questions of time use are vital ones; we miss so much just because we don't plan. If we structure our week, we save time for those extra premium things we long to do.
List the tasks to be done for the week and then place importance on each one. Complete the tasks in order of importance.

LESSON 9   Q, M, V, APOSTROPHE   MODULE I   1-25

Pronoun Agreement

DRILL 6

PRONOUN AGREEMENT

1. Review the "Pronoun Agreement (Person, Gender, Number)" section of Appendix C.
2. For each sentence, select the correct pronoun from the two choices shown in parentheses.
3. Key just the correct pronoun for each sentence.
4. Save and close. (*com-drill6*)

1. Each student must have (his or her, their) own data disk.
2. Several students have (his or her, their) own computer.
3. All candidates must submit (his or her, their) resume.
4. Napoleon organized (his, their) armies.
5. The company presented (its, their) five-year plan.
6. Jane and Alfredo sent (his and her, their) contribution.
7. Neither Chris nor Joseph wants to do (his, their) share.
8. Someone was talking on (his or her, their) cell phone and not watching the road.
9. Everybody should find a technique for stress management that works well for (him or her, them).
10. The department heads notified (his/her, their) faculty of the impending deadline.

Commas

DRILL 7

COMMAS

1. In the "Punctuation" section of Appendix C, review the "Commas" subsection.
2. Key the sentences, correcting the commas.
3. Proofread and correct errors.
4. Save and close. (*com-drill7*)

1. The legislators voted on Policy #2083 on May 23 2015 at 5 p.m.
2. To view Michelle's entire social networking site I need her permission.
3. The parents volunteered to bring coffee juice milk and pastries.
4. Several club members designed an attractive logo and the fundraising committee created an online store for selling merchandise displaying the logo.
5. Mr. Rankin explained "Upload your essay to the class blog by Monday at 9 a.m."
6. The independent film festival will be held in Baton Rouge Louisiana on May 11-15.
7. Chef Nate I appreciate your answering my questions about organic gardening on your blog.
8. Dr. Wei Li who is a visiting lecturer was selected to keynote the fall faculty convocation.
9. "Although this donut is gluten free" the nutritionist explained "it is delicious."
10. The summer teaching institute Dr. Graham was a most engaging rigorous project.

COMMUNICATION SKILLS

Lesson 9R Review

Warmup Lesson 9Ra Warmup

all reaches 1 Quij produces both fine work and excellent volume.
g/? 2 Did he go? Where is Gianna? Did George go golfing?
b/p 3 Paul has pictures of bears, bats, pigs, and bison.
easy 4 Paige is to go in a taxi to the address we stated.

Skill Building

9Rb Improve Techniques

1. Key each line once.
2. Keep your eyes on the copy.

Work for smoothness, not speed.

Apostrophe 5 I'll she'll o'clock we're didn't she's isn't don't
6 one's job; Donnel's, gov't, it's time; p's and q's
7 Spell out it's, doesn't, can't, gov't, and she'll.
q 8 netiquette queue quench quad FAQ quotes quit quest
9 Quen asked a question; eat a quince; make it quick
10 Quotes on quotas of useful equipment are required.
v 11 voice invert evoke vital prove event vacuum valid
12 improve best speed; strive high; have clear vision
13 Dev found five favorite websites for French class.

9Rc Timed Writing

1. Take two 1' timings on paragraph 1. If you finish before time is up, begin again.
2. Take a 2' timing on both paragraphs.

Goal: 13 gwam

wordwrap   gwam 1' 2'

Drill practice is a good thing to do to help with   10 | 5
speed and control. To get the most out of practice, 20 | 10
use the drills that help with the most common   30 | 15
problems. Finger and row drills are often used. Work 40 | 20
is often needed with the first, second, third, and   50 | 25
fourth fingers and rows. Work on the use of the shift 61 | 31
for capital letters as needed.   67 | 34

Work with double letters and letters next to each   10 | 39
other, as these letters often cause problems in   20 | 43
words. Spacing can also be a major concern, so   29 | 48
practice in the use of the space bar will help. Be   39 | 53
sure to review the required drills, and work on what 50 | 59
seems to help the most.   54 | 61

DRILL 4

COMPOSITION

1. DS the paragraph, inserting a proper noun in each blank and applying correct capitalization and number expression.
2. Proofread and correct errors.
3. Save and close. (com-drill4)

last _____, my friend _____ and I had a holiday, so we decided to make the most of our day and take a bicycle trip to _____. before leaving, we stopped at _____ to purchase some high-energy foods to sustain us on our trip. we packed our saddle bags and left about _____ o'clock, traveling _____ on _____ street. although we were not on a sight-seeing trip, we did pass _____ and _____. by _____ p.m., we returned home exhausted from our journey of _____ miles.

Pronoun Case

DRILL 5

PRONOUN CASE

1. Review the "Pronoun Case Agreement" section of Appendix C.
2. For each sentence, select the correct pronoun from the two choices shown in parentheses.
3. Key just the correct pronoun for each sentence.
4. Save and close. (com-drill5)

1. Was it Jane and (her, she) who starred in the movie?
2. The players who were injured were Dominique and (I, me).
3. With (who, whom) will you serve as an intern?
4. Our instructor invited (they, them) to the meeting.
5. (Who, Whom) will referee the game tonight?
6. Pat and (me, I) will be the pet sitters for Andy.
7. The problem with the delivery was between Joe and (they, them).
8. Lea and (he, him) had the highest scores on the test.
9. They bought expensive gifts for JoAnn and (I, me).
10. It was (her, she) who answered the phone.
11. Do you know to (who, whom) I should address this reference letter?
12. (My, mine) three best friends still remember my birthday every year.
13. The children invited (their, they) friends and grandparents.
14. Where do you safeguard (you, your) passwords?
15. The best painting was submitted by Carol and (her, she).

COMMUNICATION SKILLS

1a-13

Lesson 10 Z, Y, Quotation Mark, Tab

Warmup Lesson 10a Warmup

all letters 1 Quill owed those back taxes after moving to Japan.
spacing 2 Didn't Vi, Max, and Quaid go? Someone did; I know.
q/v/m 3 Marv was quite quick to remove that mauve lacquer.
easy 4 Lana is a neighbor; she owns a lake and an island.

New Keys

10b Learn z and y

z Reach *down* with *left fourth* finger.

y Reach *up* with *right first* finger.

Curve the little finger tightly to reach down and in for the z key.

z

5 za za zap zap zing zig zag zoo zed zip zap zig zed
6 doze zeal zero haze jazz zone zinc zing size ozone
7 ooze maze doze zoom zarf zebus daze gaze faze adze

y

8 y yj yj jay jay hay hay lay nay say days eyes ayes
9 yj ye yet yen yes cry dry you rye sty your fry wry
10 ye yen bye yea coy yew dye yaw lye yap yak yon any

10c All Reaches Learned

11 Did you say Liz saw any yaks or zebus at your zoo?
12 Relax; Jake wouldn't acquire any favorable rights.
13 Has Zack departed? Alex, Joy, and I will go alone.

10d Improve Keystroking
Key each line once.

14 Cecilia brings my jumbo umbrella to every concert.
direct reach 15 John and Kim recently brought us an old art piece.
16 I built a gray brick border around my herb garden.
17 sa ui hj gf mn vc ew uy re io as lk rt jk df op yu
Adjacent reach 18 In Ms. Lopez' opinion, the opera was really great.
19 Polly and I were joining Walker at the open house.

DRILL 2

CAPITALIZATION

1. Key the paragraphs, correcting all errors in capitalization.
2. Proofread and correct errors.
3. Save and close. (*com-drill2*)

as you requested, this past week i visited the facilities of the magnolia conference center in isle of palms, south carolina. bob bremmerton, group manager, was my host for the visit.

magnolia offers many advantages for our johns and lovett Leadership training conference scheduled for june 25-27. The prices are reasonable; the facilities are excellent; and the location is suitable. In addition to the beachfront location, tennis and golf packages are part of the group price.

Number Expression

DRILL 3

NUMBER EXPRESSION

1. Review the "Number Expression" section of Appendix C.
2. Key each sentence, correcting the number expression errors.
3. Proofread and correct errors.
4. Save and close. (*com-drill3*)

1. Address the letter to 1 Elm Street and postmark by April 15th.
2. The retirement reception will be held on the 1st of May in Room Twelve at 5 o'clock.
3. Program participants included fifteen supervisors, five managers, and two vice presidents.
4. 12 boxes arrived damaged and about 2/3 of the contents were crushed.
5. The manager reported that 85% of the project was complete with 9 days remaining until the March 15th due date.
6. The presiding officer called the meeting to order at two p.m. and requested that the 2 50-page reports be distributed.
7. Nearly 10 million people visited the virtual museum this year.
8. Jim lives at nine 10th Street and works on 21st Avenue.
9. The attorney quoted from Section two of the code.
10. The parents of the Twin Cities Futbol Club have raised about 50 percent of the money for the tournament.
11. Please turn to page twenty-five of the first proposal.
12. The new branding event is the 12th of November at 4 o'clock in the afternoon.
13. His baby sister weighed seven pounds nine ounces.
14. The cashier loaned the customer twenty-five cents.
15. My new address is 2 West Lawrence Street.

COMMUNICATION SKILLS

New Keys

10e Learn " (quotation mark) and TAB

" Left shift; then reach to the *right* with the *right fourth* finger.

TAB Reach *up* with *left fourth* finger.

" (quotation mark)

20 ";"; " " "web" "media" "videos" I like "texting."
21 "I am not," she said, "going." I just said, "Why?"

TAB key

22   The tab key is used for indenting paragraphs and aligning columns.
23   Tabs that are set by the software are called default tabs, which are usually a half inch.

Skill Building

10f Build Skill

Key each line once. Tap TAB to indent each paragraph. Use wordwrap, tapping ENTER only at the end of each paragraph.

24   The expression "I give you my word," or put another
25 way, "Take my word for it," is just a way I can say, "I
26 prize my name; it clearly stands in back of my words."
27 I offer "honor" as collateral.
tab 28   Tap the tab key and begin the line without a pause to maintain fluency.
29   She said that this is the lot to be sent; I agreed with her.
30   Tap Tab before starting to key a timed writing so that the first line is indented.

10g Timed Writing

Take two 1' timed writings. If you finish before time is up, begin again.

Goal: 15 gwam

E ALL LETTERS

wordwrap gwam 1'

Tab → All of us work for progress, but it is not   9
always easy to analyze "progress." We work hard for 19
it; but, in spite of some really good efforts, we may 29
fail to get just exactly the response we want.   39

Tab → When this happens, as it does to all of us, it 9
is time to cease whatever we are doing, have a quiet 20
talk with ourselves, and face up to the questions   29
about our limited progress. How can we do better?   39

| 1 | 2 | 3 | 4 | 5 | 6 | 7 | 8 | 9 | 10 |

LESSON 10 Z, Y, QUOTATION MARK, TAB   MODULE 1   **1-28**

Communication Skills

This section presents a review and quick check of basic communication skills including capitalization, number expression, pronouns, commas, subject–verb agreement, spelling, proofreading, and composition.

Capitalization

DRILL 1

CAPITALIZATION

1. Review the "Capitalization" section of Appendix C.
2. Key the sentences, correcting all capitalization errors.
3. Proofread again to ensure that you did not make any other keying errors. Correct any errors you find.
4. Save and close. (*com-drill1*)

1. according to one study, the largest ethnic minority group online is hispanics.
2. the american author mark twain said, "always do right; this will gratify some people and astonish the rest."
3. the grand canyon was formed by the colorado river cutting into the high-plateau region of northwestern arizona.
4. the president of russia is elected by popular vote.
5. the hubble space telescope is a cooperative project of the european space agency and the national aeronautics and space administration.
6. the train left north station at 6:45 this morning.
7. the trademark cyberprivacy prevention act would make it illegal for individuals to purchase domains solely for resale and profit.
8. consumers spent $7 billion online between november 1 and december 31, 2016, compared to $3.1 billion for the same period in 2015.
9. new students should attend an orientation session on wednesday, august 15, at 8 a.m. in room 252 of the perry building.
10. the summer book list includes *where the red fern grows* and *the mystery of the missing baseball.*
11. the parents brought beautiful chinese souvenirs back from their trip to shanghai.
12. the invitation was extended to governor phillip holmes and professor amanda t. wynn.
13. is this the correct capitalization for a complimentary close with two words: sincerely yours?
14. how do you capitalize the following side heading in a report: reports of standing committees?

Lesson 11 Review

Warmup Lesson 11a Warmup

alphabet 1 Zeb had Jewel quickly give him five or six points.
" (quote) 2 Can you spell "chaos," "bias," "bye," and "their"?
y 3 Ty Clay may envy you for any zany plays you write.
easy 4 Did he bid on the bicycle, or did he bid on a map?

Skill Building

11b Improve Keystroking

Work for smoothness, not speed.

5 za za zap az az maze zoo zip razz zed zax zoa zone
6 Liz Zahl saw Zoe feed the zebra in an Arizona zoo.

7 yj yj jy jy joy lay yaw say yes any yet my try you
8 Why do you say that today, Thursday, is my payday?

9 xs xs sax ox box fix hex ax lax fox taxi lox sixes
10 Roxy, you may ask Jay to fix any tax sets for you.

11 qa qa aqua quail quit quake quid equal quiet quart
12 Did Enrique quietly but quickly quell the quarrel?

13 fv fv five lives vow ova van eve avid vex vim void
14 Has Vivi, Vada, or Eva visited Vista Valley Farms?

11c Build Skill

Key balanced-hand words quickly and as phrases to increase speed.

15 is to for do an may work so it but an with them am
16 am yam map aid zig yams ivy via vie quay cob amend

17 to do is for an may work so it but am an with them
18 for it|for it|to the|to the|do they|do they|do it

19 Pamela may go to the farm with Jan and a neighbor.
20 Rod and Ty may go by the lake if they go downtown.

To apply font and font size formats:

1. Select the text; then click the down arrow to display font and font size options.
2. Click the desired font and font size. Note that 11-point Calibri is the default font.
3. To increase the font size, click A with the up arrow; to decrease the font size, click A with the down arrow.

DRILL 5

1. Key the sentences below; do not apply formats.
2. Select the words that have formatting and apply the appropriate format.
3. Save and close. (*wp-drill5*)

Change the font to Calibri Light (Heading); select **16-point text size**.

Change the font to Arial and reduce the font size to **14 points**.

Paragraph Formats

The Paragraph group contains a number of commands that can be used to format paragraphs. In this section, the focus is on the alignment commands.

❶ Align Left—all lines begin at the left margin.
❷ Center—all lines are centered.
❸ Align Right—all lines end at the right margin.
❹ Justify—all lines are aligned at the left and right margins.

Right-aligned text

Centered Text

Left-aligned text is the most frequently used alignment. All lines begin at the left margin. The right margin is uneven when text is aligned at the left side.

Justify aligns text at both the left and the right margins. All lines are even on both sides except that the last line of a paragraph may be shorter and will not end at the right margin. The system allocates additional space as needed to force the right margin to align evenly.

To apply alignment formats:

1. Click in a single paragraph or select multiple paragraphs to which a format is to be applied.
2. Click the format to be applied.

DRILL 6

1. Key the document shown above; do not format as you key.
2. Click in each paragraph and apply the alignment formats shown above.
3. Select *Centered Text*; then apply bold and increase the font size to 14 points.
4. Save and close. (*wp-drill6*)

11d Improve Techniques

Key each line once.

Key smoothly without looking at fingers.

```
       21  Make the return snappily
       22  and with assurance; keep
enter  23  your eyes on your source
       24  data; maintain a smooth,
       25  constant pace as you key.
```

When spacing, use a down-and-in motion.

```
space bar  26  us me it of he an by do go to us if or so am ah el
           27  To enter the website, key "Guest" as the password.
```

Press Caps Lock key to toggle on or off.

```
caps lock  28  Use ALL CAPS for items such as TO, FROM, or SUBJECT.
           29  Did Kristin mean Kansas City, MISSOURI, or KANSAS?
```

11e Timed Writing

Take two 1' timed writings. If you finish before time is up, begin again. The dot above words represents 2 *gwam*.

Goal: 16 *gwam*

wordwrap   gwam 1' 2'

```
    Have we thought of communication as a kind        8   4
of war that we wage through each day?                16   8
    When we think of it that way, good language      24  12
would seem to become our major line of attack.       34  17
    Words become muscle; in a normal exchange or in  43  22
a quarrel, we do well to realize the power of words. 53  27
```

11f Build Skill

1. Go to Skill Builder 1 on page 1-35.
2. Read the technique tip in the left column; concentrate on using the techniques listed.
3. Key Drill 1a from page 1-35. Key each line once, striving for good accuracy.

Text Formats

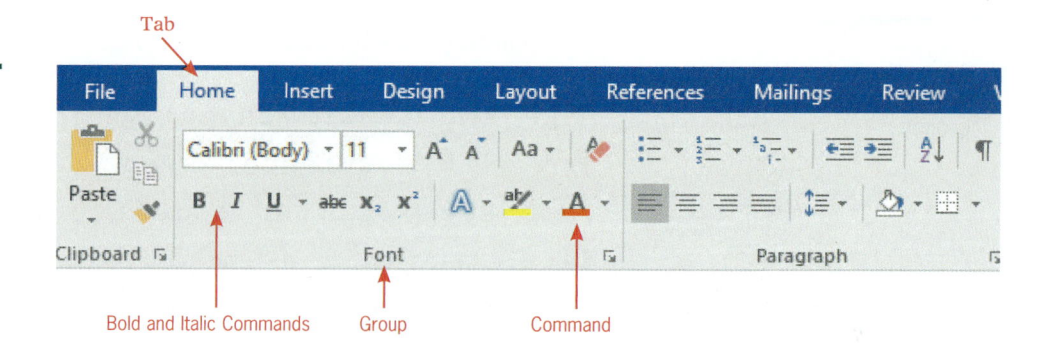

Tabs—located at the top of the Ribbon. The Home tab is selected as shown by the blue text color. Each tab displays different commands when selected.

Groups—contain a number of related commands. Logical names are positioned at the bottom of the Ribbon below each group of commands. See the Font group.

Commands—the icons, the boxes for entering information, and the drop-list menus that provide a variety of options. The Font Color command identified changes the color of text—in this case to red. The small drop-list arrow next to the Font Color command displays the colors available.

Note that commands in the Font group can be applied by selecting the text and then clicking the desired command. A good way to learn about each command is to position the mouse pointer over the command and review the screen tip. If the command has a down arrow next to it, click it to see the available options.

To apply bold, italic, or font color:

1. Select the text.
2. Click either Bold or Italic.

   – Or –

3. Click the down arrow next to the Font Color command and select the desired color.

DRILL 4

Note: in the remaining drills, you will be directed to Save and close documents with the file name shown in parentheses. See step 3. Save all drills in the Word *Processing Drills* folder.

1. Key the sentence below; do not apply formats.
2. Select the words that have bold, italic, or font color changes and apply the format shown. For color, use colors in the Standard Colors group.
3. Save and close. (*wp-drill4*)

This sentence illustrates *italic*, **bold**, and dark red font color formats.

Jane's book, *Joy of Volunteering*, won the National Volunteer Award.

Tom wore a purple costume.

Lesson 12 Review

Warmup Lesson 12a Warmup

alphabet 1 Jack won five quiz games; Brad will play him next.
q 2 Quin Racq quickly and quietly quelled the quarrel.
z 3 Zaret zipped along sizzling, zigzag Arizona roads.
easy 4 Did he hang the sign by the big bush at the lake?

Skill Building

12b Improve Keystroking

b/f
5 bf bf fab fab ball bib rf rf rib rib fibs bums bee
6 Did Buffy remember that he is a brass band member?

z/y
7 za za zag zig zip yj yj jay eye day lazy hazy zest
8 Liz amazed us with the zesty pizza on a lazy trip.

q/u
9 qa qa quo qt. quit quay quad quarm que uj jug quay
10 Where is Quito? Qatar? Boqueirao? Quebec? Quilmes?

v/m
11 vf vf valve five value mj mj ham mad mull mass vim
12 Vito, enter the words vim, vivace, and avar; save.

all
13 I faced defeat; only reserves saved my best crews.
14 In my opinion, I need to rest in my reserved seat.

all
15 Holly created a red poppy and deserves art awards.
16 My pump averages a faster rate; we get better oil.

Keep fingers curved and body aligned properly.

12c Improve Techniques

Key each line once.

de/ed
17 ed fed led deed dell dead deal sled desk need seed
18 Dell dealt with the deed before the dire deadline.

ol/lo
19 old tolls doll solo look sole lost love cold stole
20 Old Ole looked for the long lost olive oil lotion.

op/po
21 pop top post rope pout port stop opal opera report
22 Stop to read the top opera opinion report to Opal.

we/ew
23 we few wet were went wears weather skews stew blew
24 Working women wear sweaters when weather dictates.

New Document

TIP

Shortcut: To go directly to a new *Word* document when you launch *Word*, tap ESC or tap ENTER.

[New] You have already opened a new blank document when you launched *Word*. If you are already working in *Word*, you can create a new document by using the New command.

To create a new *Word* document:

1. Click the File tab, then click New.
2. Click the Blank document icon to open a new document.

Print

[Print] Print displays the printing options next to the File menu and provides a preview of the document on the right side of the screen.

To print a document:

1. On the File menu, click New; then click Print. Note the settings that are available. You will be able to use the default settings for the documents you print.
2. Preview the document.
3. Select the printing options desired.
4. Click Print.

DRILL 3

1. Open a new document and key your name on the first line; then key **wp-drill3** on the second line.
2. Key the information shown below.
3. Preview and print the document.
4. Save in your Word Processing Drills folder and close. (*wp-drill3*)

This document demonstrates the things I have learned about Word. I now can create and name folders and documents, save documents in folders, open existing documents, and print them.

Format Documents

Text and paragraphs are formatted using the commands on the Ribbon by clicking the Home tab. The first step in formatting text is to select the text.

To select text:

- Move the I-beam pointer to the beginning of the text you wish to select and click the left mouse button.
- Drag the mouse over the text to highlight it. The selected text is highlighted.

12d Improve Techniques

Key each line once.

Keep hands quiet; do not bounce. Keep fingers curved and upright.

25 a for we you is that be this will be a to and well
26 as our with I or a to by your form which all would
27 new year no order they so new but now year who may

28 This is Lyn's only date to visit their great city.
29 I can send it to your office at any time you wish.
30 She kept the fox, owls, and fowl down by the lake.

31 Harriette will cook dinner for the swimming teams.
32 Annette will call at noon to give us her comments.
33 Johnny was good at running and passing a football.

12e Timed Writing

1. Take a 2' timed writing. If you finish before time is up, begin again.
2. Use wordwrap.

Goal: 16 *gwam*

E ALL LETTERS

Copy Difficulty

What factors determine whether copy is difficult or easy? Research shows that difficulty is influenced by syllables per word, characters per word, and percent of familiar words. Carefully controlling these three factors ensures that speed and accuracy scores are reliable—that is, increased scores reflect increased skill.

In Level 1, all timings are easy. Note "E" inside the triangle at left of the timing. Easy timings contain an average of 1.2 syllables per word, 5.1 characters per word, and 90 percent familiar words. Easy copy is suitable for the beginner who is mastering the keyboard.

	gwam	2'
There should be no questions, no doubt, about	5	35
the value of being able to key; it's just a matter	10	40
of common sense that today a pencil is much too slow.	15	45
Let me explain. Work is done on a keyboard	19	49
three to six times faster than other writing and	24	54
with a product that is a prize to read. Don't you	29	59
agree?	29	60

2' | 1 | 2 | 3 | 4 | 5 |

12f Build Skill

1. Go to Skill Builder 1 on page 1-35.
2. Focus on using good techniques.
3. Key Drill 1b from page 1-35. Key each line once, striving for good accuracy.

LESSON 12 REVIEW

DRILL 1

1. Launch *Word* and open a blank document.
2. In the new document, key your name; then tap ENTER and key the text below.
3. Save the document on your computer or a flash drive in a folder named Word Processing Drills; name the document *wp-drill1*.
4. Leave the document open. (*wp-drill1*)

An effective way to manage files is to create folders to store related documents. Always name folders and files logically. Typically, folder names are formatted using initial caps, and file names using lowercase.

Close Document

If you have only one document open and you click the Close button at the upper-right side of the screen, you will close the document and exit *Word*. If you have more than one document open, only the document will close.

Clicking the Close command on the File menu closes the document and keeps *Word* open.

To close a document and leave *Word* open:

1. Click the File tab.
2. Click the Close command on the File menu.

Open Existing Document

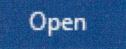

Existing documents can be opened in two ways. When you launch *Word*, recent documents will display in the left pane of the opening screen.

If you are working in *Word*, you can open existing documents not listed as recent documents by using the Open command on the File menu.

To open an existing document:

1. Click File, Open, and then This PC in the Places pane.
2. Click the Browse icon and select the folder in which you have stored the document.
3. Double-click the document name or select it and click Open.

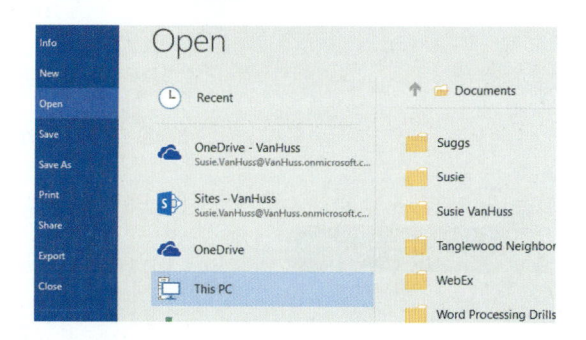

DRILL 2

1. Close the open document. (*wp-drill1*)
2. Open *wp-drill1* and on the line below your name, key **wp-drill2**. (*Note*: Text to be keyed is set off in bold; do not apply bold.)
3. Save in your Word Processing Drills folder and close. (*wp-drill2*)

WORD PROCESSING

1a-7

Lesson 13 Review

Warmup Lesson 13a Warmup

alphabet 1 Bev quickly hid two Japanese frogs in Mitzi's box.
shift 2 Jay Nadler, a Rotary Club member, wrote Mr. Coles.
, (comma) 3 Jay, Ed, and I paid for plates, knives, and forks.
easy 4 Did the amendment name a city auditor to the firm?

Skill Building

13b Improve Fluency

Key each line once.

Key short, familiar words as units.

5 is to for do an may work so it but an with them am
6 Did they mend the torn right half of their ensign?
7 Hand me the ivory tusk on the mantle by the bugle.

Key more difficult words by letter.

8 only state jolly zest oil verve join rate mop card
9 After defeat, look up; gaze in joy at a few stars.
10 We gazed at a plump beaver as it waded in my pool.

Use variable speed; your fingers will feel the difference.

11 it up so at for you may was but him work were they
12 It is up to you to get the best rate; do it right.
13 Sami greeted reporters as stars got ready at home.

13c Improve Keystroking

14 Pat appears happy to pay for any supper I prepare.
15 Knox can relax; Alex gets a box of flax next week.
16 Vi, Ava, and Viv move ivy vines, leaves, or stems.
17 It's a question of whether they can't or won't go.
18 Did Jane go? Did she see Sofia? Who paid? Did she?
19 Ms. E. K. Nu and Lt. B. A. Walz had the a.m. duty.
20 "Who are you?" he asked. "I am," I said, "Jayden."
21 Find a car; try it; like it; work a price; buy it.

Save Document in New Folder

TIP

To save to a flash drive, use the same steps shown in this activity except for step 2.

In step 2, scroll down and click Removable disk (or the name of your flash drive). Note the removable disk drive shown below.

To save a document in a new folder:

1. Click File and then click Save As.
2. Double-click the place in which to store the document, such as This PC; then click Documents to display the Save As dialog box.
3. Click the New folder button to create a new folder in which to store the document. The New folder name box displays in blue.
4. Click in the New folder name box and key the name, **Word Processing Drills**.
5. Click open or double-click the new folder (*Word Processing Drills*) to open it.

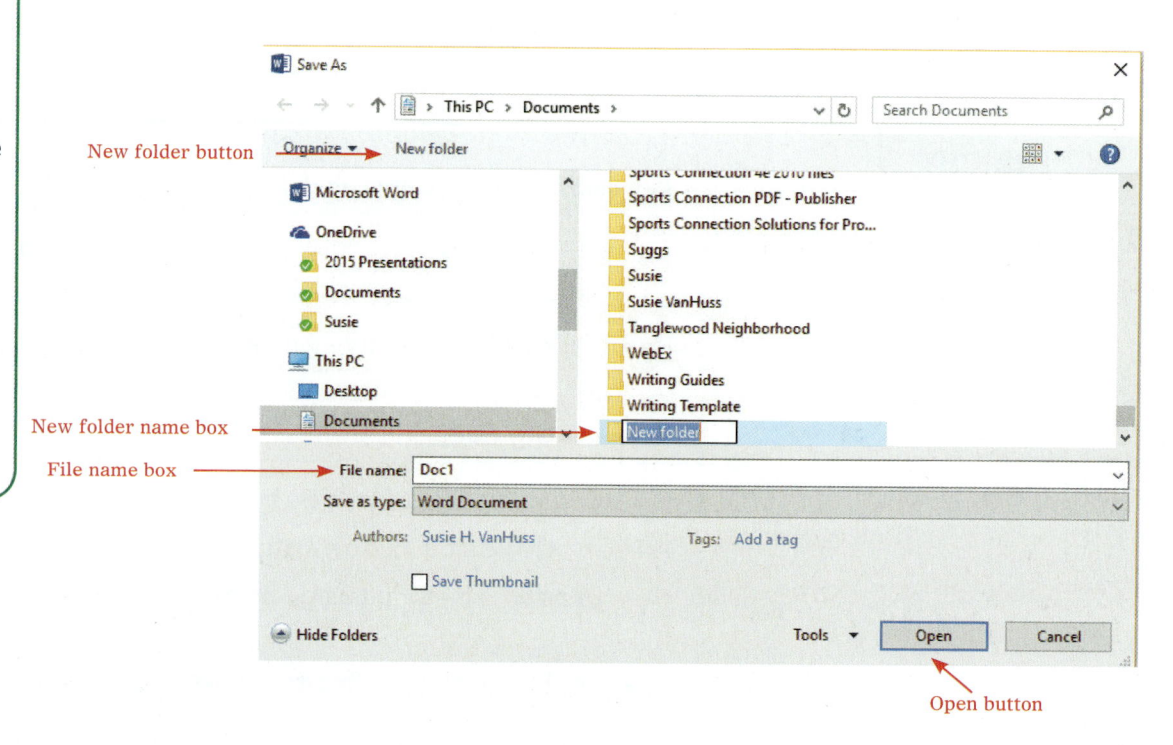

6. In the File name box, select Doc1 and key the name of the file, such as *wp-drill1*.
7. Click Save.

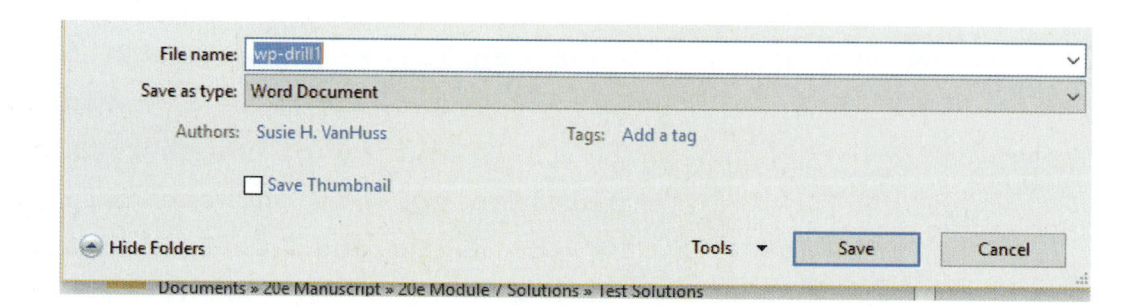

WORD PROCESSING

1a-6

13d Master Difficult Reaches

Key each line once.

Keep hands and arms still as you reach up to the third row and down to the first row.

```
t   22  at fat hat sat to tip the that they fast last slat
r   23  or red try ran run air era fair rid ride trip trap
t/r 24  A trainer sprained an arm trying to tame the bear.

m   25  am me my mine jam man more most dome month minimum
n   26  no an now nine once net knee name ninth know never
m/n 27  Many men and women are important company managers.

o   28  on or to not now one oil toil over only solo today
i   29  it is in tie did fix his sit like with insist will
o/i 30  Joni will consider obtaining options to buy coins.

a   31  at an as art has and any case data haze tart smart
s   32  us as so say sat slap lass class just sassy simple
a/s 33  Disaster was averted as the steamer sailed to sea.

e   34  we he ear the key her hear chef desire where there
i   35  it is in tie did fix his sit like with insist will
e/i 36  An expression of gratitude for service is desired.
```

13e Timed Writing

Take two 2' timed writings. If you finish before time is up, begin again.

Goal: 16 gwam

E ALL LETTERS

wordwrap   gwam 2'

```
Some people think that the first impression made       5
in the first few seconds is the best method to find   10
out what a person is like. Think of meeting friends   15
for the first time. Was this true of them? In some    20
cases, one might be correct in judging a person in a  26
few seconds. However, in most cases, one will find    31
that it takes more than the first meeting to know     36
what a person is like. But the first time meeting a   41
person could give some idea, often if a person does   46
not show good qualities. For example, one might see   51
poor speaking skills, improper dress, and poor        56
personal traits when meeting a person for the first   61
time.                                                 62
```

2' | 1 | 2 | 3 | 4 | 5 |

LESSON 13 REVIEW   MODULE 1   1-34

Managing Files in *Word*

Managing files refers to saving documents in an organized manner so that they can be easily located and used again.

[File] The File tab located in the upper-left corner of the document screen provides you with all of the commands that you need to work with files. When you click the File tab, the options for things you can do to a document display, such as open, close, save, or print.

- Commands are on the left pane. The left arrow in the circle at the top takes you back to your open document.
- Places for storing documents are shown in the middle pane.
- Recent documents are shown in the right pane.
- Click the File tab any time you want to use a command to work with files.

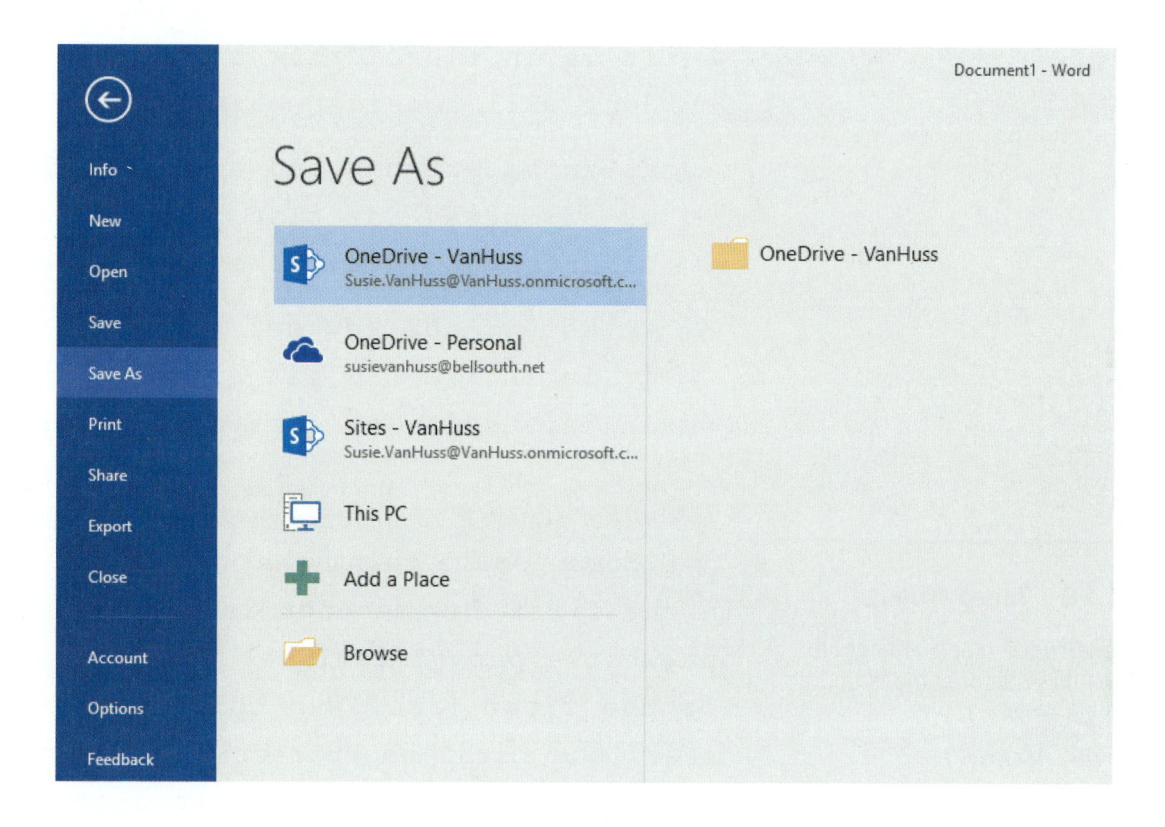

The Save and Save As commands on the File menu preserve documents for future use.

- Save is used to save a document with the same name.
- Save As is used to save a document with a name for the first time, with a different name, or to a different place.

New folders can be created from the Save As dialog box.

> **TIP**
>
> The default in *Word 2016* is to save the document to your OneDrive. Therefore, you may need to select the appropriate place on your computer or flash drive when you save folders or documents.

WORD PROCESSING

1a-5

Skill Builder 1

Skill Building *Emphasis on Improving Techniques*

For each drill, key each line once at a comfortable rate. Tap ENTER at the end of each line. Single-space the drill. Concentrate and key accurately. Repeat if desired.

DRILL 1

Goal: reinforce key locations

Key each line once at a comfortable, constant rate.

TECHNIQUE TIP

Keep
- your eyes on source copy
- your fingers curved, upright
- your wrists low but not touching
- your elbows hanging loosely
- your feet flat on the floor

Drill 1a

A We saw that Alan had an alabaster vase in Alabama.
B My rubber boat bobbed about in the bubbling brook.
C Ceci gave cups of cold cocoa to Rebecca and Rocco.
D Don's dad added a second deck to his old building.
E Even as Ellen edited her document, she ate dinner.
F Our firm in Buffalo has a staff of forty or fifty.
G Ginger is giving Greg the eggs she got from Helga.
H Hugh has eighty high, harsh lights he might flash.

Drill 1b

I Irik's lack of initiative is irritating his coach.
J Judge J. J. Jore rejected Jeane and Jack's jargon.
K As a lark, Kirk kicked back a rock at Kim's kayak.
L Lucille is silly; she still likes lemon lollipops.
M Milt Mumm hammered a homer in the Miami home game.
N Ken Linn has gone hunting; Stan can begin canning.
O Jon Soto rode off to Otsego in an old Morgan auto.
P Philip helped pay the prize as my puppy hopped up.
Q Quiet Raquel quit quoting at an exquisite marquee.

Drill 1c

R As Mrs. Kerr's motor roared, her red horse reared.
S Sissie lives in Mississippi; Lissa lives in Tulsa.
T Nat told Betty not to tattle on her little sister.
U Ula has a unique but prudish idea on unused units.
V Eva visited every vivid event for twelve evenings.
W We watched as wayworn wasps swarmed by the willow.
X Tex Cox waxed the next box for Xenia and Rex Knox.
Y Ty says you may stay with Fay for only sixty days.
Z Hazel is puzzled about the azure haze; Zack dozes.

Blank Document Screen

1. The document title, *Document1*, displays at the top center. When you save the document, you will give it a new name.

2. The Ribbon Display Options, Minimize or Maximize button, and Close button appear in the upper-right corner of the screen. If your *Word* screen does not open large enough to fill the computer screen, enlarge it by clicking the Maximize button.

Ribbon Display Options   Minimize   Maximize   Close

3. A row of tabs displays in the upper-left corner, beginning with the File tab and then the Home tab. These tabs are part of the Ribbon. To display the commands on the Ribbon, click the Ribbon Display Options button, shown with the red arrow below, and select Show Tabs and Commands. See the Ribbon with the Home tab commands displayed.

4. The center portion is the document screen on which you will key your documents. It resembles a blank sheet of paper. The insertion point indicates the position at which you will begin to key.

Note the commands on the Home tab are used to format text and paragraphs. In this brief orientation, you will learn how to apply a few basic commands to format text and paragraphs. After you complete this course, you are encouraged to continue with *Keyboarding and Word Processing Essentials* (ISBN 9781337103022) for more in-depth *Word* instruction.

WORD PROCESSING

1a-4

DRILL 2

Goal: strengthen up and down reaches

Keep hands and wrists quiet; fingers well curved in home position; stretch fingers up from home or pull them palmward as needed.

home position
1. Hall left for Dallas; he is glad Jake fed his dog.
2. Ada had a glass flask; Jake had a sad jello salad.
3. Lana Hask had a sale; Gala shall add half a glass.

down reaches
4. Did my banker, Mr. Mavann, analyze my tax account?
5. Do they, Mr. Zack, expect a number of brave women?
6. Zach, check the menu; next, beckon the lazy valet.

up reaches
7. Prue truly lost the quote we wrote for our report.
8. Teresa quietly put her whole heart into her words.
9. There were two hilarious jokes in your quiet talk.

DRILL 3

Goal: strengthen individual finger reaches

1st finger
1. Bob Mugho hunted for five minutes for your number.
2. Juan hit the bright green turf with his five iron.
3. The frigates and gunboats fought mightily in Java.

2nd finger
4. Dick said the ice on the creek had surely cracked.
5. Even as we picnicked, I decided we needed to diet.
6. Kim, not Mickey, had rice with chicken for dinner.

3rd/4th finger
7. Pam saw Roz wax an aqua auto as Lex sipped a cola.
8. Wally will quickly spell Zeus, Apollo, and Xerxes.
9. Who saw Polly? Pax Zais saw her; she is quiet now.

DRILL 4

Goal: strengthen special reaches

Emphasize smooth stroking. Avoid pauses, but do not reach for speed.

adjacent reaches
1. Falk knew well that her opinions of art were good.
2. Theresa answered her question; order was restored.
3. We join there and walk north to the western point.

direct reaches
4. Barb Nunn must hunt for my checks; she is in debt.
5. In June and December, Irvin hunts in Bryce Canyon.
6. We decided to carve a number of funny human faces.

double letters
7. Anne stopped off at school to see Bill Wiggs cook.
8. Edd has planned a small cookout for all the troop.
9. Keep adding to my assets all fees that will apply.

| 1 | 2 | 3 | 4 | 5 | 6 | 7 | 8 | 9 | 10 |

SKILL BUILDER I

Opening *Word* Screen

Note the following parts of the screen:

Left pane—contains a list of recently created documents and an option to open other documents that you may have created. If this is the first time you have used *Word*, no documents may be listed.

Main pane—provides the option to create a new blank document or create a document using one of the templates. At the upper-right side of this pane, your name will appear with either a picture or blank icon. If your Windows Live account has a picture, it will automatically appear at the top of your documents. Click the Blank document icon to begin working in *Word*.

Status bar—appears at the bottom of the screen.
On the left side, information about the document, the Windows key, the Ask me anything search box, and the Start icons for any open applications display.
The right side provides information about the layout of the document, the zoom, the time, and the date as well as information about your system.

Blank Document

The opening screen displays when you launch *Word*. To display the document screen, click the Blank document icon in the main pane. This screen is also referred to as the New document screen because you use it to create new documents.

WORD PROCESSING

1a-3

DRILL 5

Goal: improve troublesome pairs

Use a controlled rate without pauses.

1 ad add did does dish down body dear dread dabs bad
d/k 2 kid ok kiss tuck wick risk rocks kayaks corks buck
3 Dirk asked Dick to kid Drake about the baked duck.

4 deed deal den led heed made needs delay he she her
e/i 5 kit kiss kiln kiwi kick kilt kind six ribs kill it
6 Abie had neither ice cream nor fried rice in Erie.

7 fib fob fab rib beg bug rob bad bar bed born table
b/v 8 vat vet gave five ever envy never visit weave ever
9 Vic and Bev gave five very big baby beds to a vet.

10 aft after lift gift sit tot the them tax tutu tyro
t/r 11 for far ere era risk rich rock rosy work were roof
12 In Toronto, Ruth told the truth about her artwork.

13 jug just jury judge juice unit hunt bonus quiz bug
u/y 14 jay joy lay you your only envy quay oily whey body
15 Willy usually does not buy your Yukon art in July.

DRILL 6

Goal: fluency

1 Dian may make cocoa for the girls when they visit.
2 Focus the lens for the right angle; fix the prism.
3 She may suspend work when she signs the torn form.
4 Augment their auto fuel in the keg by the autobus.
5 As usual, their robot did half turns to the right.
6 Pamela laughs as she signals to the big hairy dog.
7 Pay Vivian to fix the island for the eighty ducks.

DRILL 7

Goal: eyes on the copy

1. Key sentences 1–5 for fluency. Press ENTER after each line.
2. Take a 20" and then a 30" timed writing on each sentence.

Goal: Try to key 2–3 words more on the second timing on each line.

	words	30"	20"
1 Did she make this turkey dish?		12	18
2 Blake and Laurie may go to Dubuque.		14	21
3 Signal for the oak sleigh to turn right.		16	24
4 I blame Susie; did she quench the only flame?		18	27
5 She turns the panel dials to make this robot work.		20	30

SKILL BUILDER I

Word Processing

Word 2016

Before you begin this section, review Appendix A, *Windows 10*. This section is designed to provide a brief orientation to using Microsoft® *Word 2016*. You will learn to:

- Launch *Word*
- Open, name, and close documents
- Create and name folders
- Create paragraphs
- Apply basic text formats
- Apply basic paragraph formats

Launch *Word*

Word can be launched in several different ways. The first time you launch *Word*, you will probably have to click the *Word* icon on the Start screen or on the taskbar at the bottom on your desktop screen.

Windows Start Screen

The Start screen consists of a number of tiles that enable you to access applications from your computer.

To launch *Word* from the Start screen:

1. Click the Windows key on your keyboard or on the taskbar at the lower left corner of your screen.
2. Click the *Word 2016* tile to launch *Word*. If you do not find the *Word* icon, click All apps and then click *Word 2016*.

– Or –

1. Check the taskbar at the bottom of the desktop screen to locate the *Word* icon.
2. Click the *Word* icon to launch *Word*.

To pin *Word* to the taskbar:

1. Right-click the *Word* icon.
2. Click Pin to taskbar.

> ★ **TIP**
>
> Once *Word* is open, the *Word* icon displays on the taskbar. Pin it to the taskbar so that it will remain on the taskbar when *Word* is closed.

WORD PROCESSING

1a-2

Timed Writings

TO USE TIMED WRITINGS EFFECTIVELY:

1. Select the timed writing.
2. Select the paragraph and the timing length. For example,
   - Select Paragraph 1 and 1'. Key paragraph 1; if you finish before time is up, repeat the same paragraph. Always use wordwrap when keying timed writings.
   - Select Paragraph 2 and 1'. Key paragraph 2; repeat the same paragraph if you finish before time is up.
   - Select Entire Writing and 2'. Try to maintain your 1' rate. If you finish before time is up, start over, beginning with paragraph 1.

wordwrap

E ALL LETTERS

Goal: build staying power
1. Key each paragraph for fluency. Use wordwrap.
2. Key a 2' timing on both paragraphs. Use wordwrap.

Writing 1: 18 gwam

	gwam 2'
Why spend weeks with some problem when just a few quiet	6
minutes can help us to resolve it.	9
If we don't take time to think through a problem, it will	15
swiftly begin to expand in size.	18

Writing 2: 20 gwam

We push very hard in our quest for growth, and we all think	6
that only excellent growth will pay off.	10
Believe it or not, one can actually work much too hard,	16
be much too zealous, and just miss the mark.	20

Writing 3: 22 gwam

A business friend once explained to me why he was often	6
quite eager to be given some new project to work with.	11
My friend said that each new project means he has to	16
organize and use the best of his knowledge and his skill.	22

Writing 4: 24 gwam

Just don't let new words get away from you. Learn how to spell	6
and pronounce new words and when and how to use them with skill.	13
A new word is a friend, but frequently more. New words	19
must be used lavishly to extend the size of your word power.	25

2' | 1 | 2 | 3 | 4 | 5 | 6 |

SKILL BUILDER I   MODULE I   1-38

LEVEL **1a**

Applying Keyboarding Skill

Learning Outcomes

Word Processing Skills
+ To learn and apply basic word processing commands.

Communication Skills
+ To improve basic communication skills.
+ To develop proofreading and editing skills.
+ To compose and edit documents at the keyboard.

Web-Based Computing—Internet, Cloud, and Social Media
+ To search for and use Internet information efficiently.
+ To explore cloud computing and access and store documents on OneDrive.
+ To explore social media tools.

Prepare for Your Future
+ To explore critical skills needed for career success.
+ To develop soft skills for career success through applications and a capstone project.

Goal: build staying power
1. Key each paragraph for fluency. Use wordwrap.
2. Key a 2' timing on both paragraphs. Use wordwrap.

Note: The dot above text represents two words.

Writing 5: 26 gwam

gwam 2'

We usually get the best results when we know where we are going. Just setting a few goals will help us quietly see what we can do.

Goals can help measure whether we are moving at a good rate or dozing along. You can expect a goal to help you find good results.

Writing 6: 28 gwam

To win whatever prizes we want from life, we must plan to move carefully from this goal to the next to get the maximum result from our work.

If we really want to become skilled in keying, we must come to see that this desire will require of us just a little patience and hard work.

Writing 7: 30 gwam

Am I an individual person? I'm sure I am; still, in a much, much bigger sense, other people have a strong voice in thoughts I think and actions I take.

Although we are each a unique person, we work and play in organized groups of people who just do not expect us to dismiss their rules of law and order.

DRILL 5

nk-drill5

Review

1. Turn NUMLOCK on. Open the data file and save in Numeric Keypad folder.
2. Key drills. Remember to tap the TAB key after each number, and tap ENTER after keying the number in the f column. Tap ENTER twice after each group of numbers.
3. Save and close. (nk-drill5)

★ TECHNIQUE TIP

Keep fingers curved and upright over home keys. Keep right thumb tucked under palm.

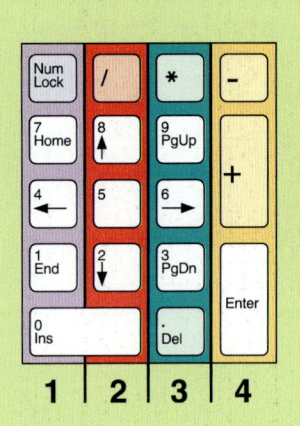

a	b	c	d	e	f
349	854	961	789	631	80
64	97	164	64	972	167
108	326	207	207	803	549
25	40	83	153	54	23
51	467	825	347	901	208
873	54	258	540	467	375
106	208	504	45	95	34
24	13	13	126	238	160
94	648	21	52	178	341
157	72	341	412	57	89
687	645	32	87	461	541
21	58	647	281	38	1,923
2,753	1,002	549	105	20	567
3,054	25	4,008	2,194	3,079	2,089
369	4,770	158	3,066	657	478
1,004	123	2,560	38	2,098	3,257
71.64	2.72	27.59	89.24	4.02	.57
285.36	118.50	438.96	102.46	55.71	6.37
3.79	24.73	4.71	527.90	.64	1.27
42.08	63.87	91.47	159.34	28.47	1.25
31.07	128.46	1.50	.28	374.95	116.00
365.87	.24	163.48	22.84	24.96	514.38
.25	394.28	452.87	349.51	852.43	234.94
147.25	32.54	821.47	164.87	.08	3.54
183.12	20.80	.60	5.07	121.07	.97

NUMERIC KEYPAD

MODULE 2

Figure and Symbol Keys

Lessons 14–18 *Figure Keys*
Lessons 19–24 *Symbol Keys*
Lesson 25 *Assessment*

LEARNING OUTCOMES

- Key the numeric keys by touch.
- Use symbol keys correctly.
- Build keying speed and accuracy.
- Apply proofreaders' marks.

Lesson 14 | 1 and 8

Warmup *Lesson 14a Warmup*

lesson 14a warmup

New Keys

14b 1 and 8

1 Reach *up* with *left fourth* finger.

8 Reach *up* with *right second* finger.

Abbreviations: Do not space after a period within an abbreviation, as in U.S., C.O.D., a.m.

The digit "1" and the letter "l" have separate values; do not interchange.

1

1 1 1a a1 1 1; 1 and a 1; 1 add 1; 1 aunt; 1 ace; 1 arm; 1 aye
2 1 and 11 and 111; 11 eggs; 11 vats; Set 11A; May 11; Item 11
3 The 11 aces of the 111th Corps each rated a salute at 1 p.m.

8

4 8 8k k8 8 8; 8 kits; ask 8; 8 kites; kick 8; 8 keys; spark 8
5 OK 88; 8 bags; 8 or 88; the 88th; 88 kegs; ask 88; order 888
6 Eight of the 88 cars score 8 or better on our Form 8 rating.

7 She did live at 818 Park, not 181 Park; or was it 181 Clark?
8 Put 1 with 8 to form 18; put 8 with 1 to write 81. Use 1881.
9 On May 1 at 8 a.m., 18 men and 18 women left Gate 8 for Rio.

14c All Figures Learned

LESSON 14 I AND 8   MODULE 2   1-40

DRILL 4

nk-drill4

Decimal

1. Turn NUMLOCK on. Open data file and save in Numeric Keypad folder.
2. Locate the decimal (.) key. It is usually located at the bottom right of the keypad.
3. Use the third finger to reach down to tap the decimal key with a quick, sharp stroke, and return to the home-key position. Keep the other fingers in the home-key position.
4. Key the drills. Remember to tap the TAB key after each number and the ENTER key after keying the number in the f column. Tap ENTER twice after each group of numbers.
5. Save and close. (nk-drill4)

★ TECHNIQUE TIP

Tap each key with a quick, sharp stroke. Release the key quickly. Keep the fingers curved and upright, the wrist low and relaxed.

a	b	c	d	e	f
.28	.19	.37	.42	.81	.96
.51	.67	.81	.27	.55	.80
.64	.50	.60	.50	.62	.43
7.10	8.91	5.64	3.12	6.04	5.01
5.32	4.27	9.21	6.47	5.28	3.24
8.94	3.06	7.38	5.89	1.37	6.78
3.62	36.94	86.73	.60	8.21	4.02
8.06	10.31	537.34	5.21	100.89	6.51
321.04	10.55	687.52	164.84	.85	207.65
.75	.26	10.85	627.98	2.57	46.51
687.46	357.95	159.46	85.21	654.32	753.15
20.46	220.48	6.10	3.04	123.54	315.47
761.64	2.82	627.25	196.25	82.99	4.02
285.46	34.60	.29	89.24	512.69	99.80
33.99	739.45	290.23	563.21	701.21	546.78
60.41	52.79	105.87	951.32	357.02	123.94
108.97	211.00	46.24	82.47	61.28	75.61
3.54	5.79	5.41	1.32	8.54	.27
.05	1.19	77.54	112.96	33.68	2.75
112.54	561.34	114.85	.24	647.21	432.89
35.67	22.01	67.90	41.08	71.28	11.00
579.21	105.24	731.98	258.96	741.21	546.21
.34	1.68	.24	.87	.63	.54
21.87	54.89	2.34	5.89	4.68	10.72

NUMERIC KEYPAD

MODULE 2

Skill Building

14d Improve Fluency

Key each line once.

Work for fluency as you key these high-frequency words.

10 a an it been copy for his this more no office please service
11 our service than the they up was work all any many thank had
12 business from I know made more not me new of some to program
13 such these two with your about and have like department year
14 by at on but do had in letter most now one please you should
15 their order like also appreciate that there gentlemen letter
16 be can each had information letter may make now only so that
17 them time use which am other been send to enclosed have will
18 Please thank the department staff for the excellent program.
19 Therefore, send the information as they are very interested.
20 She sent a receipt and an invoice for the payment due today.
21 Our board and president are happy about the new tax service.
22 We appreciate the excellent help received from every office.
23 Please return the attached form prior to the second meeting.

14e Improve Keystroking

figures

24 Our 188 trucks moved 1881 tons on August 18 and December 18.
25 Send Mary 181 No. 188 panes for her home at 8118 Oak Street.
26 The 188 men in 8 boats left Docks 1 and 18 at 1 p.m., May 1.
27 pop was lap pass slaw wool solo swap Apollo wasp load plaque
28 Was Polly acquainted with the skillful jazz player in Texas?
29 The computer is a useful tool; it helps you to perform well.

14f Build Skill

Take two 30" timed writings on each line.

Goal: Key 2 or 3 more words on the second timed writing.

30 Did their form entitle them to the land?
31 Did the men in the field signal for us to go?
32 I may pay for the antique bowls when I go to town.
33 The auditor did the work right, so he risks no penalty.
34 The man by the big bush did signal us to turn down the lane.

| 1 | 2 | 3 | 4 | 5 | 6 | 7 | 8 | 9 | 10 | 11 | 12 |

DRILL 3

nk-drill3

1, 2, 3

1. Turn NUMLOCK on. Open data file and save to Numeric Keypad folder.
2. Learn the key reaches for this drill. As you practice each reach, tap the key with a quick, sharp stroke and return to the home-key position. Keep the other fingers in the home key position.
   a. To key the number 1, reach down with the index finger.
   b. To key the number 2, reach down with the middle finger.
   c. To key the number 3, reach down with the ring finger.
3. Key the numbers for this drill. Remember to tap TAB afrer each number and tap ENTER after keying the number in the f column.
4. Tap ENTER twice after each group of numbers.
5. Save and close. (nk-drill3)

TECHNIQUE TIP

Keep fingers curved and upright over home keys. Keep right thumb tucked under palm.

a	b	c	d	e	f
11	22	33	14	15	16
41	52	63	36	34	35
24	26	25	22	42	62
27	18	39	30	20	10
30	30	10	19	61	43
32	31	21	53	83	71
414	141	525	252	636	363
141	111	252	222	363	333
111	414	222	525	333	636
111	141	222	252	366	336
152	342	624	141	243	121
330	502	331	302	110	432
913	823	721	633	523	511
702	612	513	712	802	823
213	293	821	813	422	722
24	36	15	12	32	34
115	334	226	254	346	246
20	140	300	240	105	304
187	278	347	159	357	158
852	741	963	654	321	987
303	505	819	37	92	10
28	91	37	22	13	23
524	631	423	821	922	733
15	221	209	371	300	25
823	421	24	31	19	107
652	813	211	354	231	187
50	31	352	16	210	30

NUMERIC KEYPAD

MODULE 2 1-80

Lesson 15 5 and 0

Warmup Lesson 15a Warmup

lesson 15a warmup

New Keys

15b 5 and 0

5 Reach *up* with *left first* finger.

0 Reach *up* with *right fourth* finger.

5

1 5 5f f5 5 5; 5 fans; 5 feet; 5 figs; 5 fobs; 5 frus; 5 flaws
2 5 o'clock; 5 a.m.; 5 p.m.; is 55 or less; buy 55; 5 and 5 is
3 Call Line 555 if 5 fans or 5 bins arrive at Pier 5 by 5 p.m.

0

4 0 0; ;0 0 0; skip 0; plan 0; left 0; is below 0; I scored 0;
5 0 degrees; key 0 and 0; write 00 here; the total is 0 or 00;
6 She laughed at their 0 to 0 score; but ours was 0 to 0 also.

15c All Figures Learned

7 I keyed 550 pages for Invoice 05, or 50 more than we needed.
8 Pages 15 and 18 of the program listed 150, not 180, members.
9 On May 10, Rick drove 500 miles to New Mexico in car No. 08.

Skill Building

15d Improve Keystroking

Key each line once.

Watch the copy, not the hands.

10 Read pages 5 and 8; duplicate page 18; omit pages 50 and 51.
11 We have Model 80 with 10 meters or Model 180 with 15 meters.
12 After May 18, French 050 meets in room 15 at 10 a.m. daily.

13 Barb Abver saw a vibrant version of her brave venture on TV.
14 Call a woman or a man who will manage Minerva Manor in Nome.
15 We were quick to squirt a quantity of water at Quin and West.

DRILL 2

nk-drill2

7, 8, 9

1. Turn on NUMLOCK and open the data file and save in Numeric Keypad folder.
2. Learn the key reaches for this drill. As you practice each reach, tap the key with a quick, sharp stroke and return to the home-key position. Keep the other fingers in the home key position.
   a. To key the number 7, reach up with the index finger.
   b. To key the number 8, reach up with the middle finger.
   c. To key the number 9, reach up with the ring finger.
3. Remember to tap the TAB key after keying each number, and tap ENTER after keying the number in the f column.
4. Tap ENTER after each group of numbers.
5. Save and close. (nk-drill2)

a	b	c	d	e	f
74	85	96	70	80	90
47	58	96	87	78	98
90	70	80	90	90	70
89	98	78	89	77	87
86	67	57	48	68	57
59	47	48	67	58	69
470	580	690	770	707	407
999	969	888	858	474	777
777	474	888	585	999	696
858	969	747	770	880	990
757	858	959	857	747	678
579	849	879	697	854	796
857	967	864	749	864	795
609	507	607	889	990	448
597	847	449	457	684	599
85	74	96	98	78	88
957	478	857	994	677	579
657	947	479	76	94	795
887	965	789	577	649	849
90	80	70	806	709	407
407	567	494	97	80	70
50	790	807	90	75	968
408	97	66	480	857	57
87	479	567	947	808	970
690	85	798	587	907	89
94	754	879	67	594	847
489	880	97	907	69	579

NUMERIC KEYPAD

15e Improve Techniques

Key each line once.

Build confidence—trust yourself to make the right reach.

pu/nv
16 pumps impulse campus invoices convey envy puck public canvas
17 Computer's input on environmental canvass confirms decision.

mb ey rk
18 embarked number climb eye obeying park remark thumb attorney
19 Ambitious people gambled money on unusual pieces of artwork.

tl ru pt
20 subtle apt capture excerpt adult abrupt brittle forums drug
21 Ruth opts to be greatly optimistic about seven new recruits.

ob rg un
22 objective lobster organize urge bounce tribunal global surge
23 Marge's hunger for mobile action targets frequent traveling.

15f Timed Writing

1. Take two 1' timed writings. If you finish before time is up, begin again.
2. Use wordwrap; do not tap ENTER at the end of lines.

LA ALL LETTERS

wordwrap ↓

	gwam 1'
I thought about Harry and how he worked for me in my	11
family insurance business for 10 years; how daily at 8 he	23
parked his old car in the company lot; then, he left exactly	35
at 5. Every day was almost identical for him.	44
In a quiet way, he did an outstanding job, requesting	56
little attention. So I never recognized his thirst for travel.	68
I didn't expect to find all those travel brochures near his	80
workplace.	82

1' | 1 | 2 | 3 | 4 | 5 | 6 | 7 | 8 | 9 | 10 | 11 | 12 |

Communication

15g Composition

1. Compose one paragraph that describes travel that you have done or perhaps that you wish to take. Include at least two attractions you visited or hope to visit while on this trip. Use proper grammatical structure. Do not worry about keying errors at this time.
2. Save the document as *xx-15g*. (Replace *xx* with your initials.)

LESSON 15 5 AND 0

DRILL 1

nk-drill1

4, 5, 6, 0, and ENTER

1. Turn on NUMLOCK. Open the data file and save to the Numeric Keypad folder.
2. Learn the reaches for this drill. As you practice each reach, tap the key with a quick, sharp stroke and return to the home-key position. Keep the other fingers in the home key position.
   a. To key the number 4, tap the key with the index finger.
   b. To type the number 5, tap the 5 key with the middle finger.
   c. To key the number 6, tap the 6 key with the ring finger.
   d. To key the number 0, reach down with the index finger, tap the 0 key and return to the home-key position.
   e. To move to the next line, reach down with the fourth finger, tap the ENTER key and return to the home-key position.
3. Remember to tap TAB after each number and tap ENTER after keying the number in the f column. Tap ENTER twice at the end of each group of numbers.
4. Save and close. (*nk-drill1*)

a	b	c	d	e	f
46	55	56	46	55	56
45	64	45	45	64	45
66	56	64	66	56	64
56	44	65	56	44	65
54	65	45	54	65	45
65	54	44	65	54	44
466	445	546	654	465	665
564	654	465	545	446	645
456	464	546	545	564	456
556	544	644	466	644	646
644	455	464	654	464	554
454	546	565	554	456	656
400	404	505	606	500	600
404	505	606	500	600	400
500	600	400	404	505	606
650	506	404	550	440	550
506	460	605	460	604	640
406	500	640	504	460	560
504	640	550	440	660	406
560	450	650	450	505	550
640	504	440	640	450	660
400	600	500	500	600	400
650	505	404	606	540	560
504	404	640	404	406	606

NUMERIC KEYPAD

Lesson 16 2 and 7

Warmup   Lesson 16a Warmup

lesson 16a warmup

New Keys

16b   2 and 7

2 Reach *up* with *left third* finger.

7 Reach *up* with *right first* finger.

2

1 2 2s s2 2 2; has 2 sons; is 2 sizes; was 2 sites; has 2 skis
2 add 2 and 2; 2 sets of 2; catch 22; as 2 of the 22; 222 Main
3 Exactly at 2 on April 22, the 22nd Company left from Pier 2.

7

4 7 7j j7 7 7; 7 jets; 7 jeans; 7 jays; 7 jobs; 7 jars; 7 jaws
5 ask for 7; buy 7; 77 years; June 7; take any 7; deny 77 boys
6 From May 7 on, all 77 men will live at 777 East 77th Street.

16c   All Figures Learned

7 I read 2 of the 72 books, Ellis read 7, and Han read all 72.
8 Tract 27 cites the date as 1850; Tract 170 says it was 1852.
9 You can take Flight 850 on January 12; I'll take Flight 705.

Skill Building

16d   Improve Techniques

Key each line once. Keep fingers curved and relaxed; wrists low.

3rd/4th
10 pop was lap pass slaw wool solo swap apollo wasp load plaque
11 Al's quote was, "I was dazzled by the jazz, pizza, and pool."

1st/2nd
12 bad fun nut kick dried night brick civic thick hutch believe
13 Kim may visit her friends in Germany if I give her a ticket.

3rd/1st
14 cry tube wine quit very curb exit crime ebony mention excite
15 To be invited, petition the six executive committee members.

LESSON 16   2 AND 7   MODULE 2   **1-44**

Numeric Keypad

Overview

In the lessons you completed in this text, you learned to key numbers on the 4th row of the keyboard. Many jobs require extensive use of numeric data. Using the numeric keypad on your keyboard or as a separate device is more efficient and effective than making the reaches to the 4th row to key numbers.

In this section, you will learn to use the touch system on the numeric keypad to key numbers rapidly and accurately. The most important thing to remember in using a touch system is that position—especially correct finger placement and keeping your arm parallel to the keypad–is the best way to improve speed and accuracy.

Standard Plan for Numeric Drills

Review these these steps and use them to key each drill:

1. Open the numeric keypad data file nk-drill + the drill number (nk-drill1, nk-drill2, etc.) and save it in a new folder named Numeric Keypad.
2. Read the instructions in the left column of the drill carefully.
3. Review the Numeric Keypad Layout below on the left and in the left column of the drills. The numbers at the bottom indicate the correct fingers of the right hand for each number.
4. Review the Finger Position illustration below on the right. It illustrates the correct finger position for 4, 5, and 6, which is the home row. Each drill will have an illustration showing the proper finger position.
5. Look at the numeric keypad and place your fingers over the 4, 5, and 6 keys to locate home position. All reaches are made from the home row. Move the appropriate finger up or down from home position to key a number.
6. Open the data file and key the numbers as shown in the textbook below the heading beginning with column **a**; tap the TAB key after each number is keyed to move to the next column.
7. Tap ENTER after you key the number in the last column (**f**).
8. Tap ENTER twice at the end of each group of numbers.
9. Proofread the numbers checking each against the source copy in the textbook.
10. Save and close. (nk-drill+number).

Note: Drill 4 focuses on numbers with decimals, and Drill 5 is a review to improve your mastery of keying numbers.

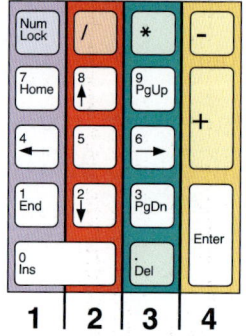

Numeric Keypad Layout

Correct Finger Position

NUMERIC KEYPAD   MODULE 2   1-77

16e Improve Keystroking

16 line 8; Book 1; No. 88; Seat 11; June 18; Cart 81; date 1881
17 take 2; July 7; buy 22; sell 77; mark 27; adds 72; Memo 2772
18 feed 5; bats 0; age 50; Ext. 55; File 50; 55 bags; band 5005
19 I work 18 visual signs with 20 turns of the 57 lenses to 70.
20 Did 17 boys fix the gears for 50 bicycles in 28 racks or 10?

16f Build Fluency
Key each line once.

Think and key the words and phrases as units rather than letter by letter.

words: *think, say, and key words*

21 is do am lay cut pen dub may fob ale rap cot hay pay hem box
22 box wit man sir fish also hair giant rigor civic virus ivory
23 laugh sight flame audit formal social turkey bicycle problem

phrases: *think, say, and key phrases*

24 is it | is it | if it is | if it is | or by | or by | or me | or me | for us
25 and all | for pay | pay dues and | the pen | the pen box | the pen box
26 such forms | held both | work form | then wish | sign name | with them

easy sentences

27 The man is to do the work right; he then pays the neighbors.
28 Sign the forms to pay the eight men for the turkey and hams.
29 The antique ivory bicycle is a social problem for the chair.

16g Timed Writing

Take two 2' timed writings. If you finish before time is up, begin again. Use wordwrap.

Goal: 16 *gwam*

gwam 2' | 3'

   When choosing a password, do not select one you have already used. Create a new one quite often, perhaps every three to four weeks. Be sure to use a combination of both letters and numbers.
   Know your password; do not record it on paper. If you must write it down, be sure the password is not recognized. Don't let anyone watch you key. Just position yourself away from the person or key a few extra strokes.

6 | 4
11 | 8
17 | 11
19 | 13
25 | 17
31 | 21
37 | 24
41 | 27

LA ALL LETTERS

2' | 1 | 2 | 3 | 4 | 5 | 6
3' | 1 | 2 | 3 | 4

LESSON E

Skill Building

> *Keep your eyes on the copy as you key each line.*

DRILL 14

Letter Combinations

Key each line once, concentrating on techniques.

br
1 bright brown bramble bread breath breezes brought brother broiler
2 In February my brother brought brown bread and beans from Boston.

exe
3 exercises exert executives exemplify exemption executed exemplary
4 They exert extreme effort executing exercises in exemplary style.

bt
5 doubt subtle obtains obtrusion subtracts indebtedness undoubtedly
6 Extreme debt will cause more than subtle doubt among my creditors.

ny
7 tiny funny company nymph penny nylon many anyone phony any brainy
8 Anyone as brainy and funny as Penny is an asset to their company.

Timed Writings

1. Take a 1' writing on each paragraph.
2. Take a 3' writing on both paragraphs at a comfortable pace.

Writing 27

	gwam	1'	3'

    Many people believe that an ounce of prevention is worth a pound   14   5
of cure. Care of your heart can help you prevent serious physical   27   9
problems. The human heart is the most important pump ever   39   13
developed. It constantly pushes blood through the body tissues. But   52   17
the layers of muscle that make up the heart must be kept in proper   66   22
working order. Exercise can help this muscle to remain in good   78   26
condition.   80   27

    Another important way to maintain a healthy heart is just by   13   31
avoiding habits which are considered to be greatly detrimental to the   27   36
body. Food that is high in cholesterol is not a good choice. Also,   41   40
use of tobacco has quite a negative effect on the function of the   54   49
heart. You can minimize your chances of heart problems by avoiding   67   54
these bad health habits.   72   55

1' | 1 | 2 | 3 | 4 | 5 | 6 | 7 | 8 | 9 | 10 | 11 | 12 | 13 |
3' | 1 | 2 | 3 | 4 |

Lesson 17 4 and 9

Warmup Lesson 17a Warmup

lesson 17a warmup

New Keys

17b 4 and 9

4 Reach *up* with *left first* finger.

9 Reach *up* with *right third* finger.

4

1 4 4f f4 f f f; if 4 furs; off 4 floors; gaff 4 fish; 4 flags
2 44th floor; half of 44; 4 walked 44 flights; 4 girls; 4 boys
3 I order exactly 44 bagels, 4 cakes, and 4 pies before 4 a.m.

9

4 9 9l l9 9 9 9; fill 9 lugs; call 9 lads; Bill 9 lost; dial 9
5 also 9 oaks; roll 9 loaves; 9.9 degrees; sell 9 oaks; Hall 9
6 Just 9 couples, 9 men and 9 women, left at 9 on our Tour 99.

17c All Figures Learned

7 4 feet; 4 inches; 44 gallons, 444 quarts, 4 folders, 44 fads
8 Lucky 99; 999 leaves; 9 lottery tickets; 9 losers; 9 winners
9 Memo 94 says 9 pads, 4 pens, and 4 ribbons were sent July 9.
10 Study Item 17 and Item 28 on page 40 and Item 59 on page 49.
11 Within 17 months he drove 85 miles, walked 29, and flew 490.

Skill Building

17d Improve Keystroking

Key each line once.

Keep hands quiet as you reach to the top row; do not bounce.

12 My staff of *18* worked *11* hours a day from May *27* to June *12*.
13 There were *5* items tested by Inspector *7* at *4* p.m. on May *8*.
14 Please send her File *10* today at *8*; her access number is *97*.
15 Car *947* had its trial run. The qualifying speed was *198* mph.
16 The estimated total score? *485*. Actual? *390*. Difference? *95*.

LESSON 17 4 AND 9 — MODULE 2 — 1-46

LESSON D

Skill Building

Keep your eyes on the copy as you key each line.

DRILL 13

Adjacent Key Review

Key each line once; at a comfortable pace.

1 nm many enmity solemn kl inkling weekly pickle oi oil invoice join
2 iu stadium medium genius lk milk talk walks uy buy buyer soliloquy
3 mn alumni hymn number column sd Thursday wisdom df mindful handful
4 me mention comment same fo found perform info le letter flew files

5 The buyer sent his weekly invoices for oil to the group on Thursday.
6 Mindful of the alumni, the choirs sang a hymn prior to my soliloquy.
7 An inmate, a fogger, and a genius joined the weekly talks on Monday.
8 They were to join in the talk shows to assess regions of the Yukon.

Timed Writings

1. Take a 1' writing on each paragraph.
2. Take a 3' writing on both paragraphs at a comfortable pace.

Writing 26

gwam 1' | 3'

All people, in spite of their eating habits, have two major needs that must be met by their food. They need food that provides a source of energy, and they need food that will fill the skeletal and operating needs of their bodies. Carbohydrates, fats, and protein form a major portion of the diet. Vitamins and minerals are also necessary for excellent health.

13 | 4
26 | 9
40 | 13
53 | 18
66 | 22
72 | 24

Carbohydrates make up a major source of our energy needs. Fats also serve as a source of energy and act as defense against cold and trauma. Proteins are changed to amino acids, which are the building units of the body. These, in turn, are utilized to make most body tissue. Minerals are required to control many body functions, and vitamins are used for normal growth and aid against disease.

12 | 28
25 | 32
38 | 37
52 | 41
64 | 45
77 | 50
84 | 52

1' | 1 | 2 | 3 | 4 | 5 | 6 | 7 | 8 | 9 | 10 | 11 | 12 | 13 |
3' | 1 | | 2 | | 3 | | 4 |

17e Improve Keystroking

first finger

17 buy them gray vent guy brunt buy brunch much give huge vying
18 Hagen, after her July triumph at tennis, may try volleyball.
19 Verna urges us to buy yet another of her beautiful rag rugs.

second finger

20 keen idea; kick it back; ice breaker; decide the issue; cite
21 Did Dick ask Cecelia, his sister, if she decided to like me?
22 Suddenly, Micki's bike skidded on the Cedar Street ice rink.

third/fourth finger

23 low slow lax solo wax zip zap quips quiz zipper prior icicle
24 Paula has always allowed us to relax at La Paz and at Quito.
25 Please ask Zale to explain who explores most aquatic slopes.

17f Timed Writing

Take a 2' timing on all the paragraphs. Repeat the timing. Use wordwrap.

LA ALL LETTERS

	gwam	2'	3'
Many experts believe stress affects the mind as well as		6	4
the body. However, they are not quite sure just how much		11	8
damage can be caused. This may be because people deal with		17	12
stress in several different ways. Some learn to either shrug		23	16
it off or else put little thought to it.		27	19
Coping with stress is difficult but if one is willing to		34	23
make an effort, it can be handled easily. One way to deal		39	27
with stress is having a good diet as well as regular exercise.		46	31
Another way is to become involved with enjoyable activities		52	35
such as writing, painting, or running. Last, but certainly not		58	39
least, have a positive thought process, a great zest for life,		64	43
and a big cheerful smile.		67	45

2' | 1 | 2 | 3 | 4 | 5 | 6 |
3' | 1 | 2 | 3 | 4 |

17g Build Skill

1. Go to Skill Builder 1 on page 1-35.
2. Key Drill 2 from page 1-36. Key each line once; strive to improve accuracy.

LESSON C

Skill Building

Work for fluency as you key these balanced-hand words.

DRILL 12

Balanced-Hand

Key each line once for fluency.

1 an anyone brand spans th their father eighth he head sheets niche
2 en enters depends been nd end handle fund or original sport color
3 ur urban turns assure to took factory photo ti titles satin still
4 ic ice bicycle chic it item position profit ng angle danger doing

5 I want the info in the file on the profits from the chic bicycle.
6 Hang the sign by the lake not by an island by six or eight today.
7 Did Vivian, the widow, pay for eight flair pens, and eight gowns?
8 When did Viviana go to the firm to sign the title to the emblems?

Timed Writings

1. Take a 1' writing on each paragraph at a fast pace.
2. Take a 3' writing on both paragraphs at a comfortable pace.

Writing 25

	gwam	1'	3'

Practicing basic health rules will result in good body condition. 14 | 5
Proper diet is a way to achieve good health. Eat a variety of foods each 29 | 10
day, including some fruit, vegetables, cereal products, and foods rich 43 | 14
in protein, to be sure that you keep a balance. Another part of a good 57 | 19
health plan is physical activity, such as running. 67 | 22

Running has become quite popular in this country. Some people 13 | 27
run for the joy of running, others run because they want to maximize 27 | 31
the benefits that can be gained by running on a regular basis. Some 41 | 36
of the benefits include weight loss, improved heart health, improved 55 | 41
bone health, and improved mood. Running is one of the most effective 68 | 45
forms of exercise that will help achieve ideal body weight. 80 | 49

SKILL BUILDER 3

Lesson 18 3 and 6

Warmup Lesson 18a Warmup

lesson 18a warmup

New Keys

18b 3 and 6

3 Reach *up* with *left second* finger.

6 Reach *up* with *right first* finger.

Note: Ergonomic keyboard users will use *left first* finger to key 6.

3

1 3 3d d3 3 3; had 3 days; did 3 dives; led 3 dogs; add 3 dips
2 we 3 ride 3 cars; take 33 dials; read 3 copies; save 33 days
3 On July 3, 33 lights lit 33 stands holding 33 prize winners.

6

4 6 6j 6j 6 6; 6 jays; 6 jams; 6 jigs; 6 jibs; 6 jots; 6 jokes
5 only 6 high; on 66 units; reach 66 numbers; 6 yams or 6 jams
6 On May 6, Car 66 delivered 66 tons of No. 6 shale to Pier 6.

18c All Figures Learned

7 At 6 p.m., Channel 3 reported the August 6 score was 6 to 3.
8 Jean, do Items 28 and 6; Mika, 59 and 10; Kyle, 3, 4, and 7.
9 Cars 56 and 34 used Aisle 9; Cars 2 and 87 can use Aisle 10.

18d Improve Fluency

Key each line once.

word response: *think* and *key* words

10 he el id is go us it an me of he of to if ah or bye do so am
11 Did she enamel emblems on a big panel for the downtown sign?

stroke response: *think* and *key* each stroke

12 kin are hip read lymph was pop saw ink art oil gas up as mop
13 Barbara started the union wage earners tax in Texas in July.

combination response: *vary speed but maintain rhythm*

14 upon than eve lion when burley with they only them loin were
15 It was the opinion of my neighbor that we may work as usual.

LESSON 18 3 AND 6   MODULE 2 1-48

LESSON B

Skill Building

Key balanced-hand words quickly and as phrases to increase speed.

DRILL 11

Balanced-Hand

Key each line once, working for fluency.

1 to today stocks into ti times sitting until ur urges further tour
2 en entire trend dozen or order support editor nd and mandate land
3 he healthy check ache th these brother both an annual change plan
4 nt into continue want of office softer roof is issue poison basis

5 Did Pamela sign the title to the big lake mansion by Lamb Island?
6 Rick is to pay the eight men and women if they do the work right.
7 My time for a land bus tour will not change until further notice.
8 I am to blame for the big problem with the maid; I can handle it.

Timed Writings

1. Key a 1' writing on each paragraph. Compare your *gwam*.
2. Key an additional 1' writing on the slower paragraph.
3. Then key both paragraphs at a comfortable pace.

Writing 24

	gwam	1'	3'

Most of us have, at some time or another, recognized an annoying 14 5
problem and had valid reasons to complain. The complaint may have 27 9
been because of a defective product, poor customer services, or 40 13
perhaps growing tired of talking to voice mail. However, many of us 54 18
feel that complaining to a business firm is an exercise in futility 67 22
so we do not bother. Instead, we just remain quiet, write it off as a 81 27
bad experience and continue to be taken advantage of. 92 31

Today, more than at anytime in the past consumers are taking some 13 35
steps to let their feelings be known—and with a great amount of 26 39
success. As a result, firms are becoming more responsive to 38 43
the needs of the consumer. complaints from customers alert firms 51 48
to produce or service defect and there by cause action to be taken 64 52
for their benefit. 68 53

SKILL BUILDER 3   MODULE 2   1-73

18e Improve Keystroking

long reaches

16 ce cede cedar wreck nu nu nut punt nuisance my my amy mystic
17 ny ny any many company mu mu mull lumber mulch br br furbish
18 Cecil received a large brown umbrella from Bunny and Hunter.

number review

19 set 0; push 4; Car 00; score 44; jot 04; age 40; Billet 4004
20 April 5; lock 5; set 66; fill 55; hit 65; pick 56; adds 5665
21 Her grades are 93, 87, and 100; his included 82, 96, and 54.

18f Timed Writing

Key two 3' writings. Use wordwrap.

gwam 3'

I am something quite precious. Though millions of people	4
in other countries might not have me, you likely do. I am very	8
powerful. I choose the new president every four years. I	12
decide if a tax should be levied or repealed. I even decide	16
questions of war and peace. I was acquired with great expense;	20
however, I am free to all citizens. But sadly enough, I am	24
often ignored; or, still worse, I am just taken for granted. I	28
can be lost, and in certain circumstances I can even be taken	33
away. What am I? I am your right to vote. Don't take me	36
lightly. Exercise your right to vote at every election;	40
consider it an opportunity and a privilege.	43

3' | 1 | 2 | 3 | 4 |

Communication

18g Composition

1. Compose two paragraphs, each having about three sentences, in which you introduce yourself to your instructor. Use proper grammatical structure. Disregard keying errors at this time.

2. Save the document as *xx-18g*; replace *xx* with your initials. You will edit this document later.

LESSON 18 3 AND 6   MODULE 2 1-49

Skill Builder 3

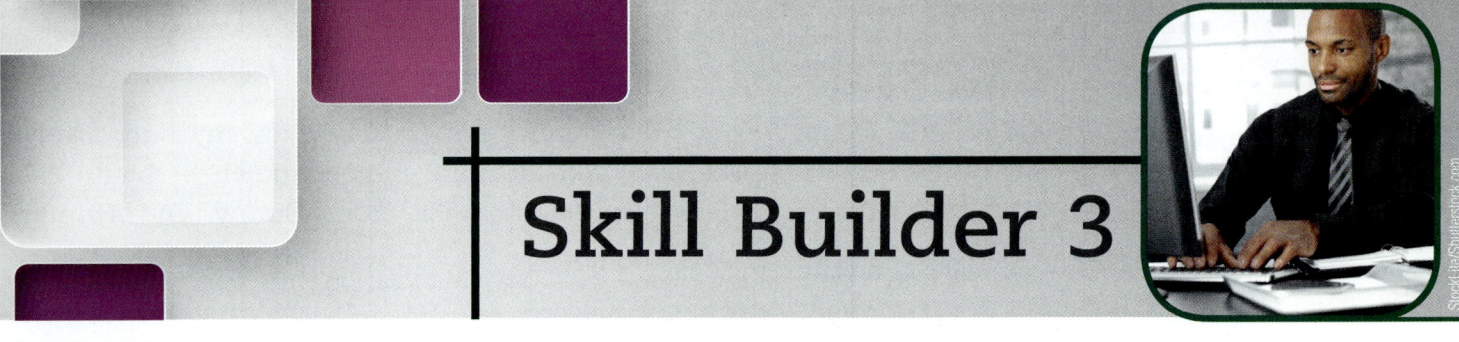

LESSON A

Skill Building

Tips for Building Speed

- Setting individual goals and striving to reach your goal is your most effective speed building strategy.
- Practice drill lines to gain confidence and fluency. Drills in Skill Builders 1, 2, and 3 are designed to build keystroking skill.
- Drills with balance-hand combinations like those on the next two pages are designed to help you key faster.
- Take short timings; then repeat them with the goal of keying two or three more words more the second time.
- After you build speed on short timings, gradually move to longer timings.

Tips for Improving Accuracy

- Relax and focus on using good techniques rather than worrying about errors.
- Make sure your arms, fingers, and feet are in the proper position.
- Strive to stroke keys fluently.
- Work for speed for short intervals and then drop back to a comfortable pace.
- At the slower speed, concentrate on one technique at a time such as keeping your eyes on the copy or minimizing hand movement.

Timed Writings

1. Key a 1' writing on each paragraph, focusing on good techniques. Compare your *gwam* on the two paragraphs.
2. Take a 1' writing on the slower paragraph, striving to exceed your speed on the faster paragraph.
3. Key both paragraphs at a comfortable pace.

Writing 23

	gwam	1'	3'

    The most valuable employees stand a greater chance of   11   4
maintaining their job in hard economic times. There are many   23   8
qualities which distinguish an excellent employee from other workers. 37 12
In the first place, they remain focused and keep their minds on the   51 17
tasks at hand. Good employees think about the work they perform and   64 21
how it relates to the total success of the project. They act as team   78 26
leaders and guide the project to completion.   87 29

    Second, good workers have the ability to work consistently and   14 33
fully realize every goal. Many people in the workplace perform just   27 38
bits and pieces of a job. They begin one thing, but allow themselves   41 42
to be quickly distracted from the work at hand. Many people are good   55 47
starters, but fewer are also good finishers.   64 50

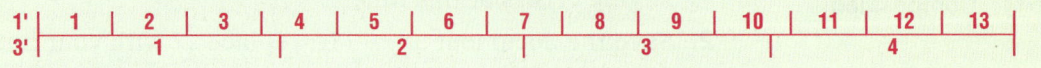

1' | 1 | 2 | 3 | 4 | 5 | 6 | 7 | 8 | 9 | 10 | 11 | 12 | 13 |
3' | 1 | 2 | 3 | 4 |

SKILL BUILDER 3   MODULE 2   1-72

Lesson 18R Review

Warmup Lesson 18Ra Warmup

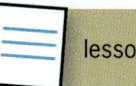

lesson 18ra warmup

Skill Building

18Rb Improve Keystroking

Key each line once; work for fluency.

1 Jake may pay the sixty men for eighty bushels of blue forks.
2 We used software versions 1.01, 2.6, 7.2, 8.3, 8.5, and 9.4.
3 The big box by the lake held fish, duck, apricot, and a map.
4 Adding 123 and 345 and 567 and 80 and 62 and 5 totals 1,182.
5 Lana and Jay and Ken paid to sit by the lake to fish at six.
6 We can see you at 6:30, 7:30, 8:45, 9:00, or 12:15 tomorrow.

18Rc Timed Writing

Key a 3' timing on all paragraphs. Repeat.

LA ALL LETTERS

gwam 3'

You want to be known as a person of good character. If   4
someone says that you have character, it usually means that   8
you are honest, have integrity, and are reliable and   12
responsible. On the other hand, if you lie, cheat, or steal,   16
or are lazy, you will be known as a person with poor   19
character. If others say that you are quite a character, it   23
usually means that you have good character.   26

You will be judged by your actions and expressions. What   30
you say and do to others affects how others will respond to   34
you. You need to be considerate of others and conscientious in   38
your work. Others will respect and trust you and want you   42
involved in their activities.   44

3' | 1 | 2 | 3 | 4 |

18Rd Improve Keystroking

1. Take a 30" timing on each line.
2. Try to maintain the same speed on each line.

7 Come work with us on this new job next month.
8 Jo will be 44 years 2 months and 24 days old.
9 I see you need some help with the new assignments.
10 I will be 44 years 2 months and 24 days old today.
11 Sixteen of us can come and help you today and tomorrow.
12 Order 99 cookies; at least have 33 sugar and 39 ginger.
13 Tell us how you want the work done; we will finish it today.
14 I delivered Order 6688 for 88 chairs and 66 tables by 6 p.m.

LESSON 18R REVIEW   MODULE 2   1-50

Writing 20

If asked, most people will agree that some people have far more creative skills than others, and they will also say that these skills are in great demand by most organizations. A follow-up question is in order. Are you born with creative skills or can you develop them? There is no easy answer to that question, but it is worth spending a good bit of time pondering.

If creative skills can be developed, then the next issue is how can you develop these skills. One way is to approach each task with a determination to solve the problem and a refusal to accept failure. If the normal way of doing a job does not work, just keep trying things never tried before until you reach a good solution. This is called thinking outside the box.

Writing 21

Figures are not as easy to key as many of the words we use. Balanced-hand figures such as 16, 27, 38, 49, and 50, although fairly easy, are slower to key because each one requires longer reaches and uses more time per stroke.

Figures such as 12, 45, 67, and 90 are even more difficult because they are next to one another and each uses just a single hand to key. Because of their size, bigger numbers such as 178, 349, and 1,220 create extra speed losses.

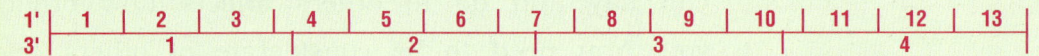

Writing 22

Few people are able to attain financial success without some kind of planning. People who realize the value of wise spending and saving are those who set up a budget. A budget will help them to determine just how much they can spend and how much they can save so that they will not squander their money recklessly.

Keeping records is a vital (~~crucial~~) part of ~~a~~ budget*ing*. A detailed records of all income and expen*ditures* (~~expenses~~) over a period of ~~a number of~~ several months will (~~can~~) help to determine what bills, like utilities (~~as water~~) or rent, are fixed (~~static~~) and which are flexible. To get the most out of your income, focus on (~~pay attention to~~) the items that you can be changed (~~modify~~).

Skill Transfer

1. Take a 2' writing on paragraph 1.
2. Take a 2' writing on paragraph 2.
3. Take 2 or more 2' writings on the slower paragraph.

Lesson 19 $ and – (hyphen)

Warmup Lesson 19a Warmup

lesson 19a warmup

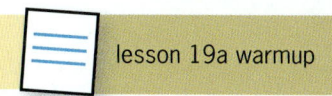

19b Learn $ and -

- = hyphen
- - = dash
Do not space before or after a hyphen or a dash.

$ Right shift; then reach *up* with *left first* finger.

- (hyphen) Reach *up* with *right fourth* finger.

$

1 $ $f f$ $ $; if $4; half $4; off $4; of $4; $4 fur; $4 flats
2 for $8; cost $9; log $3; grab $10; give Rolf $2; give Viv $4
3 Since she paid $45 for the item priced at $54, she saved $9.

- (hyphen)

4 - -; ;- - - -; up-to-date; co-op; father-in-law; four-square
5 pop-up foul; big-time job; snap-on bit; one- or two-hour ski
6 You need 6 signatures--half of the members--on the petition.

19c All Symbols Learned

7 I paid $10 for the low-cost disk; high-priced ones cost $40.
8 Le-An spent $20 for travel, $95 for books, and $38 for food.
9 Mr. Loft-Smit sold his boat for $467; he bought it for $176.

Skill Building

19d Improve Keystroking

10 Edie discreetly decided to deduct expenses in making a deal.
11 Working women wear warm wool sweaters when weather dictates.
12 We heard very rude remarks regarding her recent termination.
13 Daily sudden mishaps destroyed several dozens of sand dunes.
14 Beverley voted by giving a bold beverage to every brave boy.

Writing 17

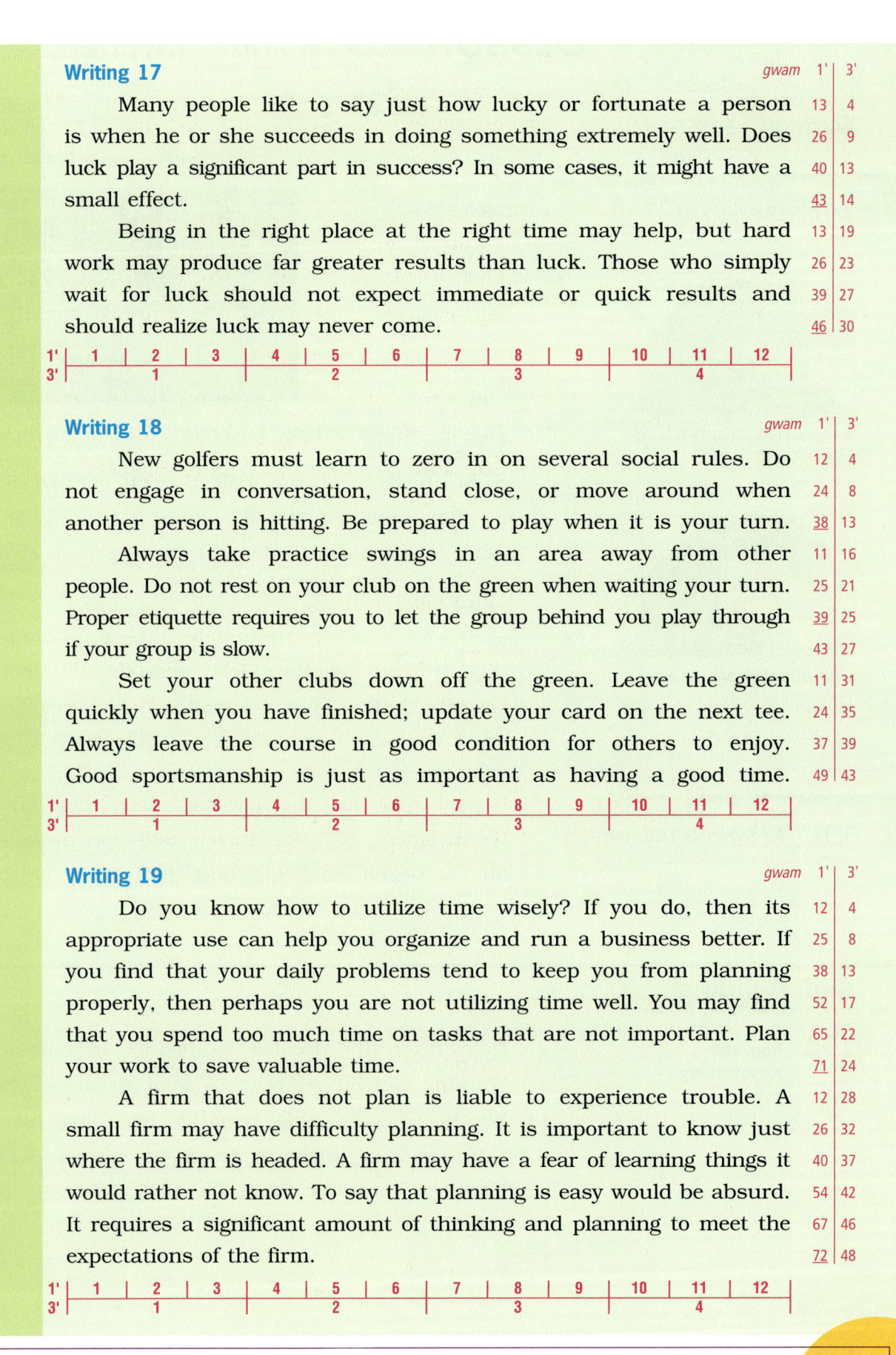

  Many people like to say just how lucky or fortunate a person is when he or she succeeds in doing something extremely well. Does luck play a significant part in success? In some cases, it might have a small effect.

  Being in the right place at the right time may help, but hard work may produce far greater results than luck. Those who simply wait for luck should not expect immediate or quick results and should realize luck may never come.

Writing 18

  New golfers must learn to zero in on several social rules. Do not engage in conversation, stand close, or move around when another person is hitting. Be prepared to play when it is your turn.

  Always take practice swings in an area away from other people. Do not rest on your club on the green when waiting your turn. Proper etiquette requires you to let the group behind you play through if your group is slow.

  Set your other clubs down off the green. Leave the green quickly when you have finished; update your card on the next tee. Always leave the course in good condition for others to enjoy. Good sportsmanship is just as important as having a good time.

Writing 19

  Do you know how to utilize time wisely? If you do, then its appropriate use can help you organize and run a business better. If you find that your daily problems tend to keep you from planning properly, then perhaps you are not utilizing time well. You may find that you spend too much time on tasks that are not important. Plan your work to save valuable time.

  A firm that does not plan is liable to experience trouble. A small firm may have difficulty planning. It is important to know just where the firm is headed. A firm may have a fear of learning things it would rather not know. To say that planning is easy would be absurd. It requires a significant amount of thinking and planning to meet the expectations of the firm.

19e Build Speed

1. Key each line once.
2. When keying easy words and phrases:
   - Think and key words and phrases rather than letter by letter.
   - Make the space part of the word.

easy words

15 am it go bus dye jam irk six sod tic yam ugh spa vow aid dug
16 he or by air big elf dog end fit and lay sue toe wit own got
17 six foe pen firm also body auto form down city kept make fog

easy phrases

18 it is | if the | and also | to me | the end | to us | if it | it is | to the
19 if it is | to the end | do you wish | to go to | for the end | to make
20 lay down | he or she | make me | by air | end of | by me | kept it | of me

easy sentences

21 Did the chap work to mend the torn right half of the ensign?
22 Blame me for their penchant for the antique chair and panel.
23 She bid by proxy for eighty bushels of a corn and rye blend.

19f Practice Numbers

1. Key lines 24–29, focusing on good techniques.
2. Key lines 24–29 again, striving for fluency.

Key numbers without watching your fingers.

24 Jan will come by at 4 o'clock to pick up the 3 girls.
25 Lauren and Paul invited 200 guests to the reception.
26 We have 3 more days to finish 66 percent of the plan.
27 Tish sent 7 24-pound boxes and 10 3-ounce envelopes.
28 I deposited 15 quarters, 10 dimes, and 4 nickels in the ATM.
29 A quorum was established; 7 of the 12 members voted.

19g Build Speed

1. Go to Skill Builder 1 that starts on page 1-35.
2. Take a 1' timed writing on Writing 2 from page 1-38.
3. Key it again. Strive to increase speed by 2 *gwam* the second time.

LESSON 19 $ AND – (HYPHEN)   MODULE 2 **1-52**

Writing 14

What do you expect when you have the opportunity to travel to a foreign country? Quite a few people realize that one of the real joys of traveling is to get a brief, but revealing glimpse of how foreigners think, work, and live.

The best way to enjoy a different culture is to learn as much about the country being visited and its culture as you can before you leave home. Then you can concentrate on being an informed guest rather than trying to find local people who can meet your needs.

Writing 15

What do you enjoy doing in your free time? Health experts tell us that far too many people choose to be lazy rather than to be active. The unpleasant result of that misguided decision shows up in our weight.

Working to control what we weigh is difficult, and seldom can it be accomplished quickly. However, it is extremely important if our weight exceeds what it should be. Part of the problem results from the amount and type of food we eat.

If we desire to appear fit, we should include exercise as a substantial component of our weight loss program. Walking at least thirty minutes each day at a very fast rate can make a major difference in our appearance and in the way we feel.

Writing 16

Doing what we enjoy doing is quite important; however, enjoying what we have to do is equally important. As you ponder both of these concepts, you may feel that they are the same, but they are quite different.

If we could do only those things that we prefer to do, the chances are that we would do them exceptionally well. Generally, we will take more pride in doing those things we thoroughly enjoy doing, and we will not stop until we get them done correctly.

We realize, though, that we cannot restrict the tasks and responsibilities that we must do just to those that we prefer to do. Therefore, we need to build an interest in and an appreciation of all the tasks that we must do in our positions.

Lesson 20 # and /

Warmup *Lesson 20a Warmup*

lesson 20a warmup

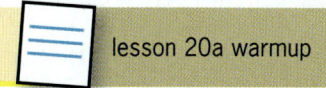

New Keys

20b Learn # and /

Right shift; then reach *up* with *left second* finger.

/ Reach *down* with *right fourth* finger.

= number sign, pounds
/ = diagonal, slash

#

1 # #e e# # # #; had #3 dial; did #3 drop; set #3 down; Bid #3
2 leave #82; sold #20; Lyric #16; bale #34; load #53; Optic #7
3 Notice #333 says to load Car #33 with 33# of #3 grade shale.

/

4 / /; ;/ / / /; 1/2; 1/3; Mr./Mrs.; 1/4/12; 22 11/12; and/or;
5 to/from; /s/ William Smit; 2/10, n/30; his/her towels; 6 1/2
6 The numerals 1 5/8, 3 1/4, and 60 7/9 are "mixed fractions."

20c All Symbols Learned

7 Invoice #737 cites 15 2/3# of rye was shipped C.O.D. 4/6/14.
8 B-O-A Company's Check #50/5 for $87 paid for 15# of #3 wire.
9 Our Co-op List #20 states $40 for 16 1/2 crates of tomatoes.

Skill Building

20d Build Skill

Strive to maintain your speed on the second line in the pair.

10 She did the key work at the height of the problem.
11 Form #726 is the title to the island; she owns it.

12 The rock is a form of fuel; he did enrich it with coal.
13 The corn-and-turkey dish is a blend of turkey and corn.

14 It is right to work to end the social problems of the world.
15 If I sign it on 3/19, the form can aid us to pay the 40 men.

16 Profit problems at the firm may cause it to take many risks.
17 Dale discovered that Invoice #238 for $128.83 is dated 8/15.

Writing 11

  Anyone who expects some day to find a great job should begin now to learn the value of accuracy. To be worth anything, final work must be correct, without question. Of course, we realize that the human aspect of the work equation always raises the chance of errors; but we should understand that those same errors can be found and fixed. Every completed job should carry at least one stamp; the stamp of true pride in work that is exemplary.

Writing 12

  No question about it: Many of the personal problems we face today arise from the fact that we have never been very wise consumers. We have not used our natural resources well; as a result, we have jeopardized much of our environment. We excused our actions because we thought that our stock of most resources had no limit at all. So, at last, we are beginning to realize just how indiscreet we were; and we are taking steps to rebuild our world.

Writing 13

  When I see people in top jobs, I know I am seeing people who sell. I am not just referring to employees who work in a retail outlet; I mean all people who put extra effort into convincing others to recognize their best qualities. They, themselves, are what they sell; and the major tools they use are their appearance, their language, and their personality. They look great, they talk and write well; and, with much self-confidence, they meet you eye to eye.

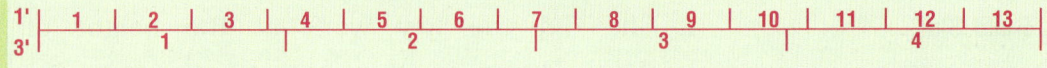

SKILL BUILDER 2

20e Build Fluency

Key each line once. Notice the difference in the rhythm of your keying.

one hand
18 lip ere him bat lion date pink face pump rear only brag fact
19 at my; oh no; add debt; extra milk; union agreed; act faster

balanced hand
20 so it is | now is the | do so when | sign the forms | is it downtown
21 He may wish to go to town with Pamela to sign the amendment.

combination
22 was for | in the case of | they were | to down | pink bowls | wet rugs
23 They were to be down in the fastest sleigh if you are right.

20f Timed Writing

1. Key a 1' timing on each paragraph; work to increase speed.
2. Key a 3' timing on all paragraphs.

LA ALL LETTERS

| | gwam | 1' | 3' |

Most people want to be socially acceptable. In some cases, the need for attention can lead to difficulties. Some of us think that the best way to get attention is to try a new style, or to look quixotic, or to be different somehow. Perhaps we are looking for nothing much more than acceptance from others of ourselves just the way we now are.

11 | 4
23 | 8
36 | 12
47 | 16
59 | 20
68 | 23

There is no question about it; we all want to look our best to impress other people. How this is achieved may mean that we try something new, or perform things differently. Regardless, our basic objective is to continue to build character with zeal from our raw materials, you and me.

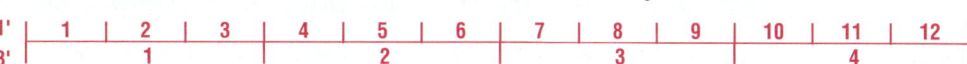

12 | 27
24 | 31
35 | 34
46 | 38
57 | 42

1' | 1 | 2 | 3 | 4 | 5 | 6 | 7 | 8 | 9 | 10 | 11 | 12 |
3' | 1 | 2 | 3 | 4 |

Communication

20g Composition

A major employer spoke at a career day at your school and indicated his company preferred to hire new employees who have had experience working in teams. He felt that teams completed projects more effectively and more efficiently than individuals and encouraged instructors to engage students in teamwork in their classes.

1. Compose a paragraph of at least three sentences describing what you think are the advantages of working on a team of four or five students to complete class projects.
2. Then compose a second paragraph of at least three sentences describing what you think are the disadvantages of working on a team of four or five students to complete class projects.
3. Save as *xx-20g*.

LESSON 20 # AND /
MODULE 2 1-54

TIMED WRITINGS

Assess Skill Growth

1. Select the writing number such as Writing 8.
2. Key 1' writings on each paragraph of a timing. Note that paragraphs within a timing increase by two words.
   Goal: to complete each paragraph
3. Key a 3' timing on the entire writing.

E ALL LETTERS

Writing 8

	gwam 1'	3'
Any of us whose target is to have success in our professional	12	4
work will understand that we must learn how to work in harmony	25	8
with others whose paths may cross ours daily.	34	11
We will, unquestionably, work for, with, and beside people, just	13	15
as they will work for, with, and beside us. We will judge them,	25	20
as most certainly they are going to be judging us.	35	23
A lot of people realize the need for solid working relations and	13	27
have a rule that treats others as they, themselves, expect to be	26	32
treated. This seems to be a sound, practical idea for them.	37	35

Writing 9

I spoke with one company visitor recently; and she was very much	13	4
impressed, she said, with the large amount of work she had noted	26	9
being finished by one of our front office workers.	36	12
I told her how we had just last week recognized this very person	13	16
for what he had done, for output, naturally, but also because of	26	21
its excellence. We know this person has that "magic touch."	38	25
This "magic touch" is the ability to do a fair amount of work in	13	29
a fair amount of time. It involves a desire to become ever more	26	34
efficient without losing quality--the "touch" all workers should	39	38
have.	40	38

Writing 10

Isn't it great just to untangle and relax after you have keyed a	13	4
completed document? Complete, or just done? No document is	25	8
quite complete until it has left you and passed to the next step.	38	13
There are desirable things that must happen to a document before	13	17
you surrender it. It must be read carefully, first of all, for	26	22
meaning to find words that look right but aren't. Read word for	39	26
word.	40	26
Check all figures and exact data, like a date or time, with your	13	31
principal copy. Make sure format details are right. Only then,	26	35
print or remove the work and scrutinize to see how it might look	39	39
to a recipient.	42	40

SKILL BUILDER 2 — MODULE 2 — 1-67

Lesson 21 % and !

Warmup Lesson 21a Warmup

lesson 21a warmup

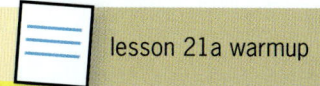

New Keys

21b % and !

% Right shift; then reach *up* with *left first* finger.

% = percent sign: Use % with business forms or where space is restricted; otherwise use the word "percent." Space once after the exclamation point.

★ TIP
- Do not space between a figure and the % or $ sign.
- Do not space before or after the dash.

% right shift; then reach up with left first finger

1 % %f f% % %; off 5%; if 5%; of 5% fund; half 5%; taxes of 5%
2 7% rent; 3% tariff; 9% F.O.B.; 15% greater; 28% base; up 46%
3 Give discounts of 5% on rods, 50% on lures, and 75% on line.

! right shift; then reach up with the left fourth finger

4 ! !a a! ! ! !; Eureka! Ha! No! Pull 10! Extra! America! Yea!
5 Attention! Now! Ready! On your mark! Get set! Go! Good show!
6 We need it now, not next week! I am sure to lose 50% or $19.

21c All Symbols Learned

7 The ad offers a 10% discount, but this notice says 15% less!
8 He got the job! With Loehman's Supermarket! Please call Mom!
9 Bill #92-44 arrived very late from Zyclone; it was paid 7/4.

21d Improve Keystroking

all symbols

10 As of 6/28, Jeri owes $31 for dinner and $27 for cab fare.
11 Invoice #20--it was dated 3/4--billed $17 less 15% discount.
12 He deducted 2% instead of 6%, a clear saving of 6% vs. 7%.

combination response

13 Look at my dismal grade in English; but I guess I earned it.
14 Kris started to blend a cocoa beverage for a shaken cowhand.
15 Jan may make a big profit if she owns the title to the land.

Skill Builder 2

Skill Building *Emphasis on Improving Techniques*

DRILL 8

Opposite Hand Reaches

Key each line once and double space (DS) between groups of lines. Key at a controlled rate; concentrate on the reaches.

i/e
1. ik is fit it sit laid site like insist still wise coil light
2. ed he ear the fed egg led elf lake jade heat feet hear where
3. lie kite item five aide either quite linear imagine brighter
4. Imagine the aide eating the pears before the grieving tiger.

w/o
5. ws we way was few went wit law with weed were week gnaw when
6. ol on go hot old lot joy odd comb open tool upon money union
7. bow owl word wood worm worse tower brown toward wrote weapon
8. The workers lowered the brown swords toward the wood weapon.

DRILL 9

Proofreaders' Marks

Key each line once and DS after each sentence. Correct the sentence as edited, making all handwritten corrections. Do not key the numbers.

≡ Capitalize
/ Change letter
⌒ Close up space
⤴ Delete
∧ Insert
lc Lowercase
\# Space
∽ Transpose

1. When a writer create the preliminary version of a document, they are concentrating on conveying the intended ideas.
2. This version of a preliminary document is called a rough.
3. After the draft is created the Writer edits refines the copy.
4. Sometimes proofreader's marks are used to edit the draft.
5. The changes will them be make to the original.
6. After the changes have been made, then the Writer reads the copy.
7. Editing and proofreading requires alot of time and effort.
8. An attitue of excellance is reqiured to produce error free message.

DRILL 10

Proofreading

Compare your sentences in Drill 9 with Drill 10. How did you do? Now key the paragraph for fluency. Concentrate on keying as accurately as possible.

When a writer creates the preliminary version of a document, he or she is concentrating on conveying ideas. This preliminary version is called a rough draft. After the draft is created, the writer edits or refines the copy. Proofreaders' marks are used to edit the rough draft. The editing changes will be made to the original. Then the writer reads the copy again. Editing requires a lot of time and effort. An attitude of excellence is required to produce an error-free message.

21e Improve Techniques

Key each line once.

1st finger

16 by bar get fun van for inn art from gray hymn July true verb
17 brag human bring unfold hominy mighty report verify puny joy
18 You are brave to try bringing home the van in the bad storm.

2nd finger

19 ace ink did cad keyed deep seed kind Dick died kink like kid
20 cease decease decades kick secret check decide kidney evaded
21 Dedre likes the idea of ending dinner with cake for dessert.

3rd finger

22 oil sow six vex wax axe low old lox pool west loss wool slow
23 swallow swamp saw sew wood sax sexes loom stew excess school
24 Wes waxes floors and washes windows at low costs to schools.

4th finger

25 zap zip craze pop pup pan daze quote queen quiz pizza puzzle
26 zoo graze zipper panzer zebra quip partizan patronize appear
27 Czar Zane appears to be dazzled by the apple pizza and jazz.

21f Timed Writing

1. Key a 1' timing on each paragraph.
2. Key a 3' timing on both paragraphs.

LA ALL LETTERS

	gwam	1'	3'
Teams are the basic unit of performance for a firm. They		12	4
are not the solution to all the problems and needs of the		24	8
organization. However, they can perform at a higher rate		35	12
compared to other groups. Their support has great impact on		47	16
changes that are crucial to a firm.		54	18
Teams are not established just by joining people together		13	22
in a group. Team members should have a clear purpose and they		25	26
should also work with each other to reach a common goal. In		37	30
order to make a quality working plan, the team must maximize		49	38
their time and their abilities. They need to learn how to help		62	39
one another and make an effort to coordinate the tasks.		73	42

1' | 1 | 2 | 3 | 4 | 5 | 6 | 7 | 8 | 9 | 10 | 11 | 12 |
3' | 1 | 2 | 3 | 4 |

21g Build Skill

Take two 1' writings; the last number you key is your approximate *gwam*.

Reach for numbers with a minimum of hand movement.

1 and 2 and 3 and 4 and 5 and 6 and 7 and 8 and 9 and 10 and 11 and 12 and 13 and 14 and 15 and 16 and 17 and 18 and 19 and 20 and 21 and 22 and 23 and 24 and 25 and 26 and 27 and

LESSON 21   % AND !

25e Figure Check

Key two 3' writings at a controlled rate. Save the timings as *xx-25e-t1* and *xx-25e-t2*. Use wordwrap.

Goal: 3', 14–16 *gwam*.

gwam 3'

Do people read the stock market pages in the news? Yes; at approximately 9 or 10 a.m. each morning, I know lots of excited people who do that. Some people still like to have the paper delivered to their home each morning. Others like the convenience of reading the news on their computer or their cell phone. Nevertheless, we can't wait to obtain the first stock report each day.

Some people take the stock market very seriously. They watch their stocks carefully and note the rise and fall of each stock. Most investors like to be able to "buy at 52 and sell at 60." Some would like to receive a dividend of 7 or 8 percent on their stocks. Regardless, each morning we zip immediately to the stock report to see how the market is doing. When the stock is down, we quickly purchase more shares and keep them until they increase in value. The stock market is an important and vital part of our life.

3' | 1 | 2 | 3 | 4 |

Communication

25f Edit Copy

1. Key your name, class, and date at the left margin.
2. Key the paragraphs and make the corrections marked with proofreaders' marks. Use the Backspace key to correct errors.
3. Save as *xx-25f*.

Last week the healthy heart foundation released the findings of a significant study that showed exercising, dieting, and not smoking are the major controllable factors that led to a healthy heart. Factors such as heredity cannot be controlled. The study included both 25 to 65 year aged males and females. women especially benefited from

The study also showed that just taking a walk. Those who walked an average of 2 to 3 hours a week were more than 30 percent less likely to have a problems than those who did no exercise.

25g Proofread and Edit

1. Open *xx-24Rd*.
2. Turn to page 1-68 and proofread your document with Writing 11.
3. Make corrections as needed. Save as *xx-25g*.

LESSON 25 ASSESSMENT MODULE 2 1-65

Lesson 22 (and) and Backspace Key

Warmup Lesson 22a Warmup

lesson 22a warmup

New Keys

22b (and)

(Left shift; then reach *up* with the *right third* finger.

) Left shift; then reach *up* with the *right fourth* finger.

( ) = parentheses
Parentheses indicate off-hand, aside, or explanatory messages.

1 ((l l((; (; Reach from l for the left parenthesis; as, ((.
2)); ;))); Reach from ; for the right parenthesis; as,)).

( )

3 Learn to use parentheses (plural) or parenthesis (singular).
4 The red (No. 34) and blue (No. 78) cars both won here (Rio).
5 We (Galen and I) dined (bagels) in our penthouse (the dorm).

22c All Symbols Learned

6 The jacket was $35 (thirty-five dollars)--the tie was extra.
7 Starting 10/29, you can sell Model #49 at a discount of 25%.
8 My size 8 1/2 shoe--a blue pump--was soiled (but not badly).

Build confidence—trust yourself to make the correct reach.

22d Improve Keystroking

Key each line once.

9 Jana has one hard-to-get copy of her hot-off-the-press book.
10 An invoice said that "We give discounts of 10%, 5%, and 3%."
11 The company paid bill 8/07 on 5/2/14 and bill 4/9 on 3/6/14.
12 The catalog lists as out of stock Items #230, #710, and #13.
13 Ellyn had $8; Sean, $9; and Cal, $7. The cash total was $24.
14 A representative from the 16th District (Tom Law) will come.
15 The oldest family member (May Gray) will attend the reunion.

Lesson 25 Assessment

Warmup Lesson 25a Warmup

lesson 25a warmup

Skill Building

25b Improve Keystroking

n/y
1 deny many canny tiny nymph puny any puny zany penny pony yen
2 Jenny Nyles saw many, many tiny nymphs flying near her pony.

b/r
3 bran barb brim curb brat garb bray verb brag garb bribe herb
4 Barb Barber can bring a bit of bran and herbs for her bread.

c/e
5 cede neck nice deck dice heck rice peck vice erect mice echo
6 Can Cedric erect a decent cedar deck? He erects nice condos.

n/u
7 nun gnu bun nut pun numb sun nude tuna nub fun null unit gun
8 Eunice had enough ground nuts at lunch; Uncle Launce is fun.

25c Improve Fluency

Key each line once.

9 is if he do rub ant go and am pan do rut us aid ox ape by is
10 it is|an end|it may|to pay|and so|aid us|he got|or own|to go
11 Did the girl make the ornament with fur, duck down, or hair?

12 us owl rug box bob to man so bit or big pen of jay me age it
13 it|it is|time to go|show them how|plan to go|one of the aims
14 It is a shame they use the autobus for a visit to the field.

25d Timed Writing

Key two 3' writings. Strive for accuracy. Save the timings as *xx-25d-t1* and *xx-25d-t2*. Use wordwrap.

Goal: 3', 19–27 gwam.

> Build confidence—trust your reach instincts.

gwam 3'

    The term career can mean many different things to 4
different people. As you know, a career is more than just an 8
occupation. It includes the jobs an individual has over time. 12
It also involves how the work life affects the other parts of 16
our life. There are as many types of careers as there are 20
people. 20

    Almost every person has a career of some kind. A career 24
can help us attain unique goals, such as having a stable 28
livelihood or a rewarding vocation. The kind of career you 32
have will affect your life in many ways. For example, it can 36
determine where you live, the money you make, and how you feel 40
about yourself. A good choice can thus help you realize the 44
life you want. 45

3' | 1 | 2 | 3 | 4 |

LESSON 25 ASSESSMENT   MODULE 2   1-64

22e Backspace Key

Key sentences 16–21: use the Backspace key to correct errors as they occur.

Use the Backspace key effectively.

Backspace   reach up with the right fourth finger

16 You should be interested in the special items on sale today.
17 If she is going with us, why don't we plan to leave now?
18 Do you desire to continue working on the memo in the future?
19 Did the firm or their neighbors own the autos with problems?
20 Juni, Vec, and Zeb had perfect grades on weekly query exams.
21 Jewel quickly explained to me the big fire hazards involved.

Skill Building

22f Timed Writing

1. Take two 3' timings on both paragraphs.
2. Use the Backspace key to correct errors.

gwam 3'

It is our obligation to preserve the planet and hand it	4
down to our children and grandchildren in a better condition	8
than when we first found it. We must take extra steps just to	12
make the quality of living better. Unless we change our ways	16
and stop damaging the environment, the world will not be a	20
good place to live.	22
To help save our ozone layer, we should not use any	25
products that may have harmful gas in them. There are many	29
simple and easy ways to clean the air such as planting more	33
trees and reusing materials. Also as important is the proper	37
disposal of our garbage in order to stop our water from	41
getting more and more polluted.	43

3' | 1 | 2 | 3 | 4 |

LESSON 22 (AND) AND BACKSPACE KEY   MODULE 2   1-58

Lesson 24R Review

Warmup   Lesson 24Ra Warmup

lesson 24ra warmup

Skill Building

24Rb Master Numbers and Symbols

Key each line once; work for fluency.

1. E-mail invoice #397 to gmeathe@skd.org; the $7 will be paid.
2. Jane and Ken may go to town to handle the pale and sick dog.
3. The answers to pop quiz #12 are: (1) a, (2) c, (3) b, (4) c.
4. Uncle Jeff rented a burgundy minivan for three days a month.
5. Check #42 was sent on 6/15 for the amount of $89 as payment.
6. Zale played amazing pop jazz on a saxophone and a xylophone.
7. L & D Bank pays 7% interest on savings accounts, 10% on CDs.

24Rc Timed Writing

1. Key a 1' timing on each paragraph; work to increase speed.
2. Key a 3' timing on all paragraphs.

	gwam 1'	3'
Do you find yourself forgetting the names of people that	12	4
you have known for quite some time? Did you put something down	25	8
and a few minutes later were not able to find it again? Memory	37	12
lapses like these are normal, and there are things you can do	50	17
to prevent them from happening as often. Just a few simple	62	21
lifestyle changes can easily help improve your memory.	72	24
Everyone can take steps to better their memory; it will	12	28
take both time and practice. It is important to get enough	24	32
sleep and to eat properly. Exercise both the mind and the	36	36
body. Read, write, and do puzzles each day to help develop	47	44
your memory. Make time for family and friends and have a good	60	48
time with them.	63	49

1' | 1 | 2 | 3 | 4 | 5 | 6 | 7 | 8 | 9 | 10 | 11 | 12
3' | 1 | | 2 | | 3 | | 4

24Rd Enrichment

1. Key the paragraphs, making revisions as you key.
2. Key your name and 24Rd below the paragraph.
3. Save as xx-24Rd.

Any one who expects someday to find an excellent job should learn the value of accuracy. To be worth any thing completed work must be accurate, without any question. Naturally we realize that the aspect of the work equation raises always the chance of errors; we should know that those same mistakes can be found and fixed. Every job completed should carry at least 1 stamp; the stamp of approval in work that is outstanding.

Lesson 23 & and : (colon), Proofreaders' Marks

Warmup Lesson 23a Warmup

lesson 23a warmup

New Keys

23b & and : (Colon)

& = ampersand: The ampersand is used only as part of company names.

Colon: Space once after a colon except when used within a number for time.

& Left shift; then reach *up* with *right first* finger.

: (colon) Left shift; then tap key with *right fourth* finger.

& (ampersand)

1 & &j j& & & &; J & J; Haraj & Jay; Moroj & Jax; Torj & Jones
2 Nehru & Unger; Mumm & Just; Mann & Hart; Arch & Jones; M & J
3 Rhye & Knox represent us; Steb & Doy, Firm A; R & J, Firm B.

: (colon)

4 : :; :; : : :; as: for example: notice: Dear Sir: Gentlemen:
5 In stock: 10:30; 7:45; Age: Address: Read: Cell: Attachment:
6 Space once after a colon, thus: Telephone: Home Address: To:

23c All Symbols Learned

7 Consider these companies: J & R, Brand & Kay, Upper & Davis.
8 Memo #88-829 reads as follows: "Deduct 15% of $300, or $45."
9 Bill 32(5)--it got here quite late--from M & N was paid 7/3.

Skill Building

23d Improve Keystroking

Key each line once.

10 Jane may work with an auditing firm if she is paid to do so.
11 Pam and eight girls may go to the lake to work with the dog.
12 Clancy and Claudia did all the work to fix the sign problem.
13 Did Lea visit the Orlando land of enchantment or a neighbor?
14 Ana and Blanche made a map for a neighbor to go to the city.
15 Sidney may go to the lake to fish with worms from the docks.
16 Did the firm or the neighbors own the auto with the problem?

Skill Building

24c Improve Keystroking

double letters
13 feel pass mill good miss seem moons cliffs pools green spell
14 Assets are being offered in a stuffy room to two associates.

balanced hand
15 is if of to it go do to is do so if to the to sign it vie to
16 Pamela or Jen may also go to town with Blanche if she works.

24d Timed Writing

Take two 3' timings.
Use wordwrap.

gwam 3'

Why do we resist change so much? Do you think perhaps it   4
is because it requires more time and effort learning new   8
things and making difficult decisions? Is it also because we 12
are set in our ways, afraid to take chances and dislike being 16
told what to do? Besides, what is the point of trying to   20
improve something that works just fine?   22

We know change can and does extend new areas of   26
enjoyment, areas we might never have known existed. If we stay   30
away from all change, we could curtail our quality of life.   34
People who are open to change are more zealous and more   38
productive than those who aren't. They are also better at   42
coping with the hardships and challenges that life often   46
brings.   46

3' | 1 | 2 | 3 | 4 |

Communication

24e Composition

1. Open the file *xx-profile* that you created in Lesson 18.
2. Position the insertion point at the end of the last paragraph. Tap ENTER twice.
3. Key an additional paragraph that begins with the following sentence:
   Thank you for allowing me to introduce myself.
4. Finish the paragraph by adding two or more sentences that describe your progress and satisfaction with keyboarding.
5. Use the Backspace key to correct errors as you key the document.

24f Edit Copy

1. Key your name, class, and date at the left margin on separate lines.
2. Key each line, making the corrections marked with proofreaders' marks.
3. Proofread and correct errors using the Backspace key.
4. Save as *xx-24f*.

17 Ask Group 1 to read Chater 6 of Book 11 (Shelf 19, Room 5).
18 All 6 of us live at One Bay road, not at 126-56th Street.
19 AT 9 a.m. the owners decided to close form 12 noon to 1 p.m.
20 Ms. Vik leaves June 9; she returns the 14 or 15 of July.
21 The 16 percent discount saves $115. A stamp costs 44 cents.
22 Elin gave $300,000,000; our gift was only 75 cents.

LESSON 24 OTHER SYMBOLS

23e Improve Keystroking

double letters

17 Do Bennett was puzzled by drivers exceeding the speed limit.
18 Bill needs the office address; he will cut the grass at ten.
19 Todd saw the green car veer off the street near a tall tree.

figures and symbols

20 Invoice #84 for $672.90, plus $4.38 tax, was due February 3.
21 Do read Section 4, pages 60–74 and Section 9, pages 198–225.
22 Enter as follows: (a) name, (b) address, and (c) cell phone.

23f Timed Writing

Take two 3' timings. Use wordwrap.

	gwam 3'
Is how you judge my work important? Does your honest	4
opinion or feedback really matter? It does, of course; I hope	8
you appreciate the effort and recognize some basic merit in	12
it. We all expect to get credit for the hard work we put forth	16
and the good work we conclude. After all, we are all working	20
together to accomplish the goals of the company.	23
As a human being, I want approval for the ideas	27
presented, things written, and tasks completed. I always look	31
forward to your evaluations so I can learn more and continue	35
to grow. My work does not define me, but it shows my abilities	39
and skills. Through my work, I am my very own unique self.	43

3' | 1 | 2 | 3 | 4 |

Communication

23g Edit Text

1. Key your name, class, and **23g** at the left margin. Then key lines 23–28, making the revisions as you key. Use the Backspace key to correct errors.
2. Proofread and correct errors.
3. Save as xx-23g.

Symbol	Meaning	Symbol	Meaning
—	Italic	sp	Spell out
~~	Bold	¶	Paragraph
Cap or ≡	Capitalize	#	Add horizontal space
∧	Insert	/ or lc	Lowercase
	Delete	⌒	Close up space
	Move to left	∼	Transpose
	Move to right	stet	Leave as originally written

23 We miss 50% in life's rewards by refusing to new try things.
24 do it now--today--then tomorrow's load will be 100%% lighter.
25 Satisfying work- whether it pays $40 or $400- is the pay off.
26 Avoid mistakes: confusing a #3 has cost thousands.
27 Pleased most with a first-rate job is the person who did it.
28 My wife and/or me mother will except the certificate for me.

LESSON 23 & AND : (COLON), PROOFREADERS' MARKS

Lesson 24 Other Symbols

Warmup Lesson 24a Warmup

lesson 24a warmup

New Keys

24b Textbook Keying

@ * + =

@	at
*	asterisk
+	plus sign (use a hyphen for minus and x for "times")
=	equals

Be confident—watch the copy, not the hands.

@ shift; reach *up* with *left third* finger to @

1 @ @s s@ a a; 24 @ .15; 22 @ .35; sold 2 @ .87; were 12 @ .95

2 You may contact Calvin @: CEP@rpx.com or fax @ 602.555.0101.

3 E-mail Al ajj@crewl.com and Matt mrw10@scxs.com by 9:30 p.m.

* shift; reach *up* with *right second* finger to *

4 * *k k8* * *; aurelis*; May 7*; both sides*; 250 km.**; aka*

5 Note each *; one * refers to page 29; ** refers to page 307.

6 Use *.* to search for files; the * looks for all characters.

+ shift; reach *up* with *right fourth* finger to +

7 + ;+ +; + + +; 2 + 2; A+ or B+; 70+ F. degrees; +xy over +y;

8 The question was 8 + 7 + 51; it should have been 8 + 7 + 15.

9 My grades on the tests and final exam are B+, C+, B+, and A.

= reach *up* with *right fourth* finger to =

10 = =; = = =; = 4; If 14x = 28, x = 2; if 8x = 16, then x = 2.

11 Change this solution (where it says "= by") to = bx or = BX.

12 Key the formula =(a2+b2)*d5/4 in the formula bar; tap Enter.

Appendix A Windows 10

START WINDOWS 10

Windows 10 is the newest operating system software released by Microsoft. The operating system software controls the operations of the computer and works with the application software. *Windows 10* works with *Word* in opening, printing, deleting, and saving files. It also allows you to work with photos, play music and videos, and access the Internet.

Some new features in *Windows 10* includes Cortana, a personal assistant. Cortana can assist you with finding files on your computer, manage your calendar, or chat with you. *Microsoft* introduced a new web browser, *Microsoft Edge*. This new default browser is faster and more secure than *Internet Explorer*. *OneDrive*, formerly called *Sky Drive*, is the online storage service that is easily accessible from *Windows 10*.

When you turn on your computer, the *Windows 10* Lock screen displays. Tap any key to display the *Windows 10* Sign-in screen. Key your password and tap ENTER to display the *Windows 10* Desktop.

Windows 10 Lock screen

Windows 10 Sign-in screen

WINDOWS 10 DESKTOP

The *Windows 10* desktop displays once the sign-in procedure is competed. The *Windows* desktop, similar to the actual top of a desk, will be the surface on which you work. You can open files and folders and place them on the desktop. When you open *Microsoft Word*, it will display on the desktop. To display the desktop from any location, press ⊞ + D. The Windows key (⊞) is located to the left of the Space Bar; it is often referred to as the WinKey. *Microsoft* provides keyboard shortcuts that make it easy for you to interface with *Windows 10*. Pressing WinKey + D is a shortcut because it quickly displays the *Windows* desktop. WinKey + E is another shortcut that opens *File Explorer*.

Refer to the illustration on the following page to familiarize yourself with the basic screen elements.

Windows to Desktop

- *Taskbar* ❶. The taskbar displays across the bottom of the window. Use the mouse to point to each item in the taskbar. Look for the ScreenTip that displays identifying each element.
    - *Start button* ❷. Click the Start button to display the Start menu. The Start menu provides access to the recently used apps, commonly used settings, and live tiles.
    - *Search box* ❸. The search box allows searches of files and folders on the computer and online.
    - *Apps and file buttons*. Buttons display for the apps that are open or pinned to the taskbar and allow you to switch between them easily. The *Task View* ❹ icon shows all open applications. The *Microsoft Edge* ❺ icon is displayed to provide quick access to the Internet. The *File Explorer* ❻ icon provides quick access to your files. The *App Store* ❼ leads to the Windows Store and access to purchase digital content including apps, games, and media.
    - *Notification Area* ❽. The notification area provides helpful information, such as the date and time and the status of the computer. When you plug in a USB drive, Windows displays an icon in the notification area letting you know that the hardware is connected.
- *Icons and Shortcuts*. Icons, small pictures representing certain items, may be displayed on the desktop. The Recycle Bin, shown as a wastepaper basket, displays when Windows is installed. Other icons and shortcuts may be added.
- *Desktop*. This is the work area where you will be working on your documents and apps.

SHUT DOWN COMPUTER

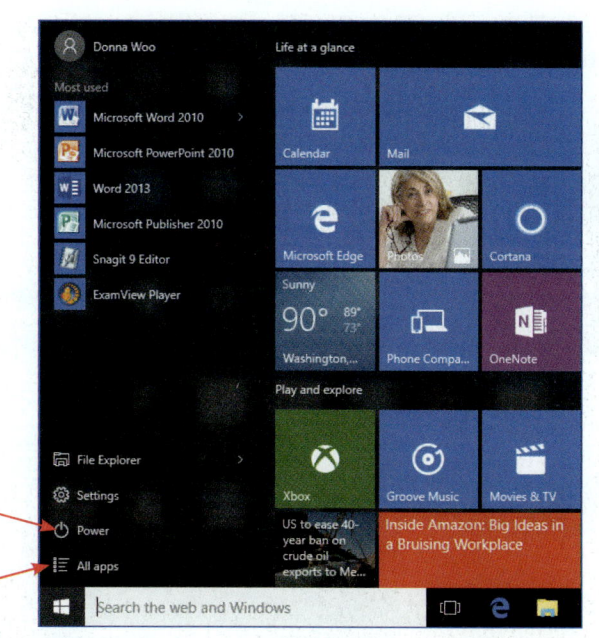

Power

All apps

Start menu

Shut down menu

1. Move your mouse pointer to the lower left of the Desktop and click Start, or tap the WinKey on your keyboard to open the Start menu. The right side of the Start menu displays application tiles. The left side of the menu displays the recently accessed apps and programs, as well as frequently accessed places on the PC. Your Start menu probably does not look identical to the illustration.
2. Click Power to display the Power options.
3. Click Shut down.

DRILL 1 — START WINDOWS

1. Sign in to *Windows 10*.
2. Click the Start button to display the Start menu.
3. Click All apps to display an alphabetical list of installed Apps. Use the vertical scroll bar to scroll down to find the Get Started tile.
4. Double-click Get Started; the *Get Started* app opens.
5. Click *Cortana* from the list on the left, then click What is *Cortana*? Read about *Cortana*, using the scroll bar to view all the information.
6. Click *Microsoft Edge* from the list on the left, then click Get to know *Microsoft Edge*. Use the scroll bar to view all the information. Close the window.
7. Click the WinKey to display the Start menu.
8. Click Power, then Shut down.

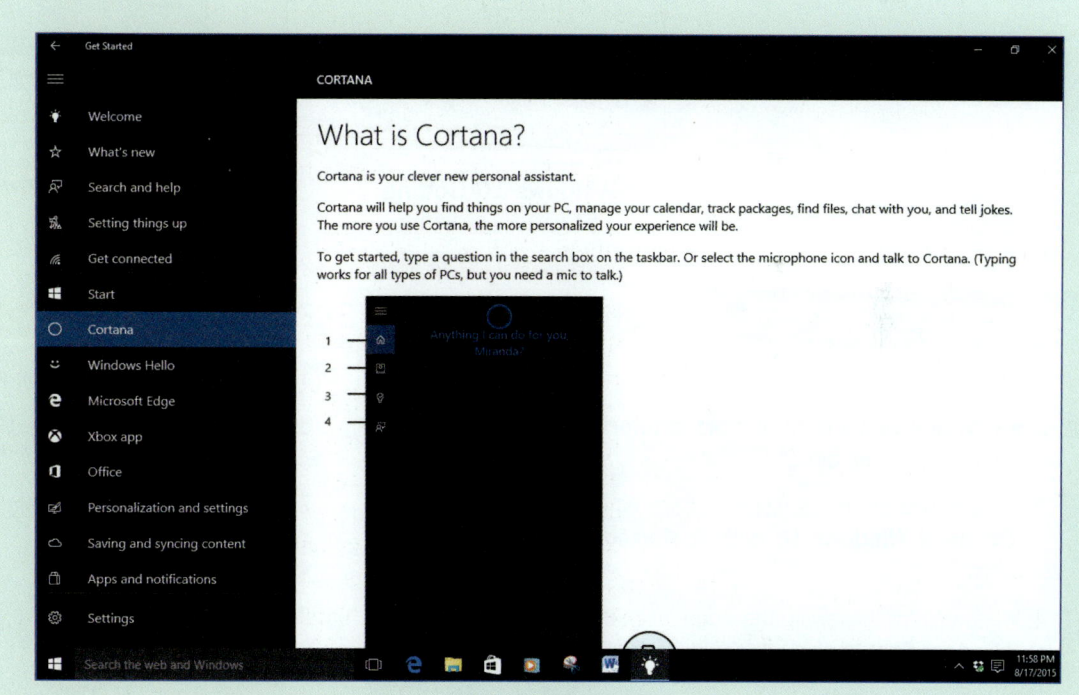

What is *Cortana*?

APPENDIX A WINDOWS 10

REF3

WINDOWS 10 HELP

The *Windows 10 Help and Support* feature contains documentation on how to use *Windows 10*; this feature is stored online. You must be connected to the Internet to access online help.

You can access Help by keying your question in the Search box located in the taskbar area. You can also access Help by tapping F1 from within Windows or any desktop program. A list of topics will display; click the link to display the information.

Windows 10 Search box

Windows 10 Getting Started Tutorials

Windows search results

DRILL 2 — USING WINDOWS HELP AND SEARCH

1. Sign in to *Windows 10*.
2. Key **Windows 10 getting started tutorials** in the *Windows 10* Search box, then tap ENTER.
3. A list of related topics displays. Click on one of the icons below **Videos of Windows 10 getting started tutorials** to view the video.
4. When you finish viewing the video, click the close button ⊠ in the upper right to close the window, then return to the Desktop.
5. Click the *File Explorer* icon in the Taskbar.
6. With the application open, tap the F1 key to display the help topics relating to *File Explorer*.
7. After viewing, close the window and return to your desktop.

APPENDIX A WINDOWS 10

REF4

Appendix B File Management

FILE EXPLORER

TIP

Expand and collapse icons may not display until the mouse moves into the left Navigation page.

Data is stored in files on the computer. To use the files, you need to know the name of the file and the location in which it is saved. *Windows 10* stores related files in folders. Folders can also be stored within folders, called subfolders. *File Explorer* provides the interface for you to manage the file system. Click the File Explorer icon on the taskbar to display the *File Explorer* window.

The left pane is the Navigation pane, which shows the drives on the computer and the files stored on each drive. If an expand icon > displays to the left of the folder or drive, that means the folder or drive contains subfolders. You can expand the list to view the subfolders by clicking the > icon. Once the list is expanded, the expand icon changes to a collapse icon; clicking the collapse icon V will hide the subfolders.

The Contents pane lists the contents of the folders. Click on a folder in the Navigation pane to display the contents of the folder in the Contents pane. If you want to get a preview of what a file looks like, click the View tab; then in the Panes group, click Preview pane to display an additional pane that shows a preview of your file.

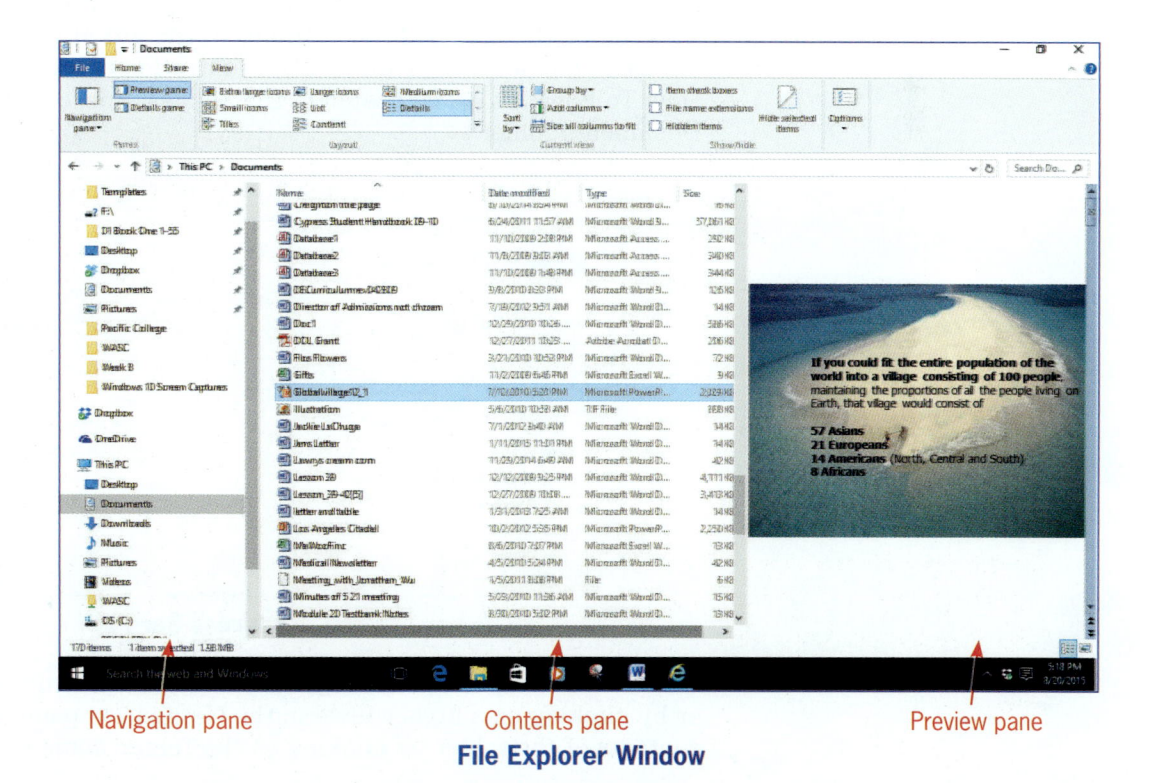

Navigation pane   Contents pane   Preview pane

File Explorer Window

When you open *File Explorer*, it displays six Quick Access areas—Desktop, Downloads, Documents, Music, Pictures, and Videos. Documents, by default, save in the Documents folder. To view the Documents folder, move the mouse over Documents in the left pane, then click the expand icon. Click the expand icon to the left of the Documents folder to display its contents.

Files can be stored in various locations or drives on the computer. To view the drives on your computer, click This PC in the Navigation pane. The drives display in the right pane. They are labeled with letters followed by a colon (C:, D:, E:). The local disk, which stores the software, is usually labeled as drive (C:). If you are using a USB drive to save your files, it is often designated as drive E: or F:.

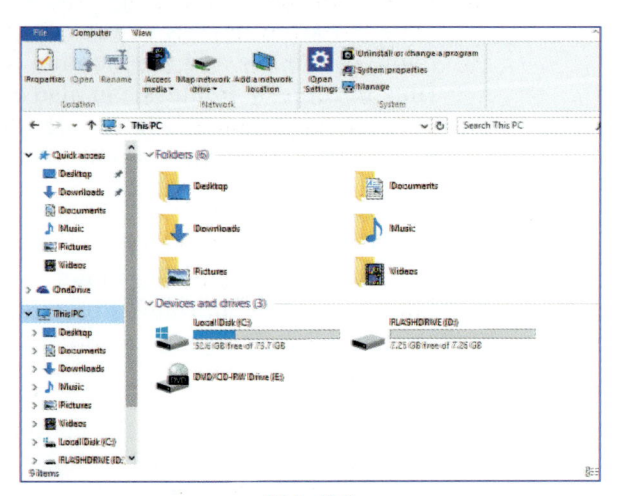

This PC

FILE ADDRESSES

The address bar, located above the Navigation and Contents pane, shows the location or address of the file. Each level of the file hierarchy is separated with a > symbol; the highest level displays at the left of the address bar. The > symbol indicates the next lower level. The illustration below shows that the selected file, How To Earn A's ❶, is located in the Success subfolder ❷, which is located in the Documents folder ❸.

Address Bar Path

You can move up the hierarchy by clicking on the higher level in the address bar or by clicking on a higher level in the Navigation pane. You can also display the contents of the folder by clicking on the folder name in the address bar.

WORK WITH FILES AND FOLDERS

Folders are extremely important in organizing files. You will create and manage folders and the files within them so that you can easily locate them. A folder can store files, or it may contain subfolders that store files. The use of folders and subfolders helps to reduce clutter so that you can find, navigate, and manage your files, folders, and disks with greater speed.

NAMING FILES

Good file organization begins with giving your folders and files names that are logical and easy to understand. A filename should be meaningful and reflect the contents of the file. Filenames can be up to 255 characters long, but in practice you will not use filenames that long. In addition, the following symbols cannot be used in a filename: \ / : * ? " , . The descriptive name is followed by a period (.), which is used to separate the descriptive name from the file extension. The file extension is three or four letters that follow the period. When renaming a file, do not delete or change file extensions as this may cause problems opening the file.

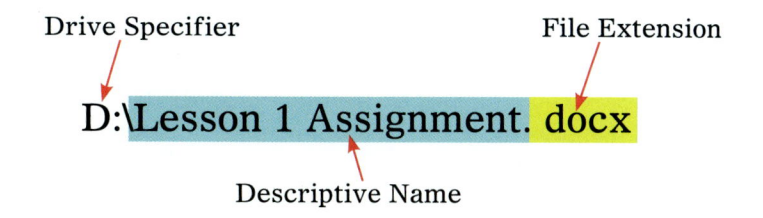

Drive Specifier → D:\Lesson 1 Assignment. docx ← File Extension

Descriptive Name

FILE EXPLORER HOME TAB

Commands that are commonly used are located on the Home tab. The Ribbon is divided into groups, similar to those of other *Microsoft Office* products. The commands to create new folders and to rename files and folders are located on the Home tab.

Home tab on the Ribbon

To create a file folder:
Home/New/New Folder

1. In the left pane of *File Explorer*, double-click the drive or folder that is to contain the new folder ❶.
2. Click the New folder command. A yellow folder icon displays in the right pane with the words *New folder* highlighted ❷.
3. Key the new folder name and tap ENTER.

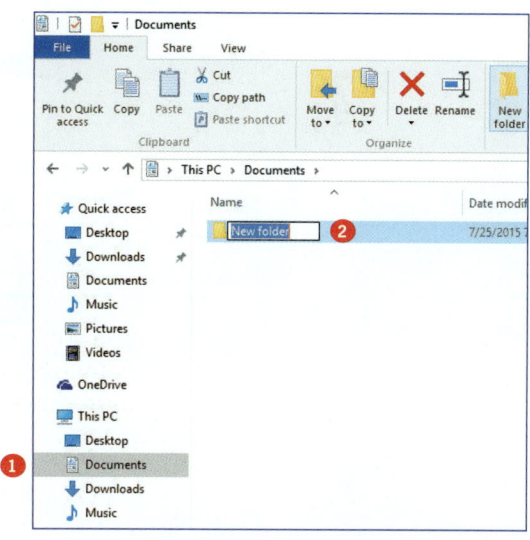

New Folder Creation

APPENDIX B FILE MANAGEMENT

To rename a file or folder:
Home/Organize/Rename

1. Access *File Explorer* and display the contents of your removable storage drive (or the location where you have been instructed to save your document files or folders).
2. Click the file or folder icon to be renamed.
3. Click Rename on the Ribbon.
4. Key the new name and tap ENTER.

COPY, MOVE, OR DELETE FILES OR FOLDERS

You can use the commands in the Organize group on the Home tab to move, copy, or delete files and folders.

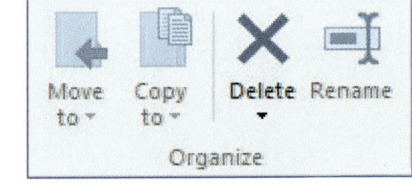

Organize Group

To move a file or folder:
Home/Organize/Move to

1. Select the file or folder to be moved.
2. Click the Move to drop-down arrow; a list of folders on your computer displays.
3. Select a location from the Move to drop-down list, *or*
4. Click Choose location to display the Move items dialog box. Select the destination and click Move.

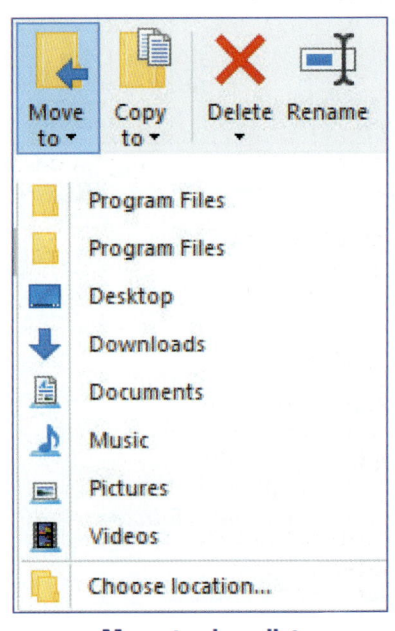

Move to drop list

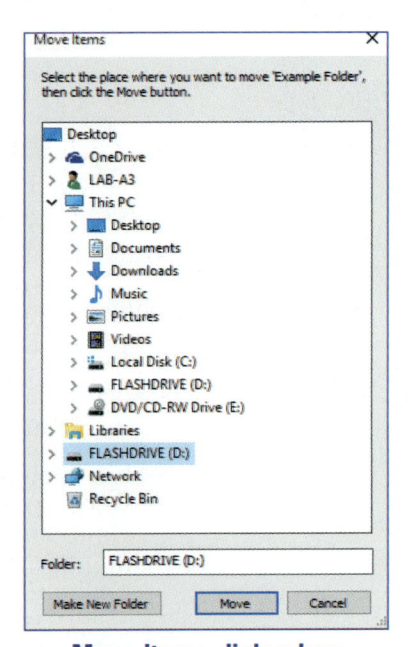

Move Items dialog box

> **TIP**
> The names of the files need to be selected from the Contents pane in order to use the commands in the Home ribbon.

APPENDIX B FILE MANAGEMENT

REF8

To copy a file or folder:
Home/Organize/Copy to

1. Select the file or folder to be copied.
2. Click the Copy to drop-down arrow to display the Copy to drop-down list.
3. Select a location from the Copy to drop-down list or click Choose location to display the Copy items dialog box. Select the location for the copy to be placed and click Copy.

To delete a file or folder:
Home/Organize/Delete

1. Select the file or folder to be deleted.
2. Click Delete.

When you delete a file or folder from the hard drive, it is not removed from the storage immediately. It moves to the Recycle Bin and remains there until the Recycle Bin is emptied. This gives you the opportunity to restore the file to its original location if you discover that it should not have been deleted.

ONEDRIVE APP

Microsoft made OneDrive an integral part of the *Windows 10* operating system by including the *OneDrive* app as part of the *File Explorer* navigation. OneDrive is a service that allows you to store documents, photos, videos, and audio files on the Microsoft servers. A benefit of storing files on OneDrive is the ability to access the files from any computer or *Windows* phone. The files can be shared with family and friends. Coworkers can collaboratively work on *Microsoft Office* documents. You need to have a Microsoft account to access OneDrive.

To access OneDrive: *(Internet connection and a Microsoft account needed.)*

1. From the *Windows 10* Desktop, open the Start menu, click All apps, and find the *OneDrive* app. Alternatively, you may access OneDrive using the navigation menu of *File Explorer*.

TIP

Updates are continually made to OneDrive. Read your screen carefully as its appearance and steps may vary over time.

2. If this is the first use of OneDrive on the computer, you may be prompted to sign in with your Microsoft account. Folders and files located on OneDrive will display; you may use these files as if they were on your computer, and changes made will synchronize to OneDrive.

3. OneDrive can be used in the same way a file or folder on your computer is used.

Welcome to OneDrive

APPENDIX B FILE MANAGEMENT

REF9

Appendix C Reference Guide

Pronoun Case Agreement

1. Use the nominative case when the pronoun is the subject of a verb.

   She enjoys reading before going to sleep.

2. Use the nominative case for a predicate pronoun following a linking verb.

   It is **she** who made the motion to adjourn.

3. Use the objective case when the pronoun is the object of a preposition.

   This information must be kept between you and **me**.

4. Use the objective case when the pronoun is a direct or an indirect object.

   He told **her** to take the subway. (direct object)
   Please send **me** Joe's address. (indirect object)

5. Use *who* in the nominative form as a subject of the sentence; use *whom* in the objective form as a direct object.

   Who is knocking at the door?
   To **whom** do I write my check?

6. Use the possessive case to show ownership.

   My sister is moving to Paris for **her** internship.

Pronoun Agreement (Person, Gender, Number)

1. A personal pronoun agrees in person, gender, and number with the noun or pronoun it represents.

   The **students** worked to pay **their** tuition.
   You worked in the summer to pay **your** tuition.

2. Indefinite pronouns such as *each, every, everyone, everything, somebody, anybody, either,* and *neither* are singular. The indefinite pronouns such as *many, both, few,* and *several* are plural.

   Each of the honorees worked to pay **his/her** tuition.
   All of the honorees had guests for **their** banquet.

3. A personal pronoun that represents a collective noun may be singular or plural, depending on the meaning of the collective noun.

   The **team** voted unanimously to keep Coach Johnson as **its** head coach. (individual action)
   The **family** are debating on **their** vacation destination this summer. (separate actions)

Subject/Verb Agreement

1. Use a singular verb with a singular subject. Use a plural verb with a plural subject.

   The **granddaughter is** loved by her grandparents.
   The **honorees are** seated at the head table.

2. Use a singular verb with singular indefinite pronouns. Use a plural verb with plural pronouns.

   Each of the honorees **works** to pay his/her tuition.
   All of the winners **work** to pay their bills. (plural)

3. Use a plural verb with a compound subject joined by *and*.

   The **students** and the **faculty attend** the meeting.

4. For subjects joined by words like *or* or *nor* use a singular verb if the subject closer to the verb is singular and plural if the subject closer to the verb is plural.

   Neither Susie nor **I is** available today.
   Either Pat or his team **members are** available.

5. Use a singular verb with a collective noun when the group acts as a unit. Use a plural verb when the members act individually.

   The **team votes** unanimously today. (singular)
   The **family are** debating their vacation. (plural)

Abbreviations

1. With a few exceptions, do not use abbreviations in general writing.

2. Spell out an abbreviation for the first use and key the abbreviation in parenthesis. For future use of the word, use the abbreviation.

   First time: National Science Foundation (NSF)
   Second and subsequent times: NSF

3. Abbreviate the names of well-known organizations and agencies with capitals and no periods.

   NSF   NATO

4. Abbreviate professional designations and academic degrees after a name.

   CPA   PhD

5. Add *s* to make most abbreviations plural. Generally to make them plural possessive, add an apostrophe.

   CPAs

6. Spell out standard units of measure in general writing; elsewhere, use abbreviations for space or readability.

   He weighs 200 pounds and is 5 feet 10 inches tall.

APPENDIX C REFERENCE GUIDE

Punctuation

Use an apostrophe

1. To make most singular nouns and indefinite pronouns possessive (add **apostrophe** and **s**).

   computer + 's = computer's   Jess + 's = Jess's
   anyone's   one's   somebody's

2. To make a plural noun that does not end in s possessive (add **apostrophe** and **s**).

   women + 's = women's   men + 's = men's
   deer + 's = deer's   children + 's = children's

3. To make a plural noun that ends in s possessive. Add only the **apostrophe**.

   boys + ' = boys'   managers + ' = managers'

4. To make a compound noun possessive or to show joint possession. Add **apostrophe** and **s** to the last part of the hyphenated noun.

   son-in-law's   Rob and Gen's game

5. To form the plural of numbers and isolated lowercase letters and the capital letters A, I, M, and U, add **apostrophe** and **s**. To show omission of letters or figures, add an **apostrophe** in place of the missing items.

   7's   A's   p's and q's   It's   '70s

Use a colon

1. To introduce a listing.

   The candidate's strengths were obvious: experience, community involvement, and forthrightness.

2. To introduce an explanatory statement.

   Then I knew we were in trouble: The item had not been scheduled.

Use a comma

1. After an introductory phrase or dependent clause.

   After much deliberation, the jury reached its decision. If you have good skills, you will find a job.

2. After words or phrases in a series.

   Mike is taking Greek, Latin III, and Chemistry II.

3. To set off nonessential or interrupting elements.

   Troy, the new man in MIS, will install the hard drive. He cannot get to the job, however, until next Friday.

4. To set off the date from the year and the city from the state.

   John, will you please reserve the center in Billings, Montana, for January 10, 2018.

5. To separate two or more parallel adjectives (adjectives could be separated by *and* instead of a comma).

   The loud, whining guitar could be heard above the rest.

6. Before the conjunction in a compound sentence. The comma may be omitted in a very short sentence.

   You must leave immediately, or you will miss your flight. We tested the software and they loved it.

7. Set off appositives and words of direct address.

   Karen, our team leader, represented us at the conference.
   Paul, have you ordered the ten dozen red roses?

Use a hyphen

1. In two-word adjectives before a noun

   two-car family

2. In compound numbers between twenty-one and ninety-nine.

3. In fractions and some proper nouns with prefixes/suffixes.

   two-thirds   ex-Governor   all-American

Use italic

1. With titles of complete literary works.

   College Keyboarding   *Hunt for Red October*

2. To emphasize special words or phrases.

   What does *professional* mean?

Use a semicolon

1. To separate independent clauses in a compound sentence when the conjunction is omitted.

   Please review the information; give me a report by Tuesday.

2. To separate independent clauses when they are joined by conjunctive adverbs (*however, nevertheless, consequently,* etc.).

   The traffic was heavy; consequently, I was late.

3. To separate a series of elements that contain commas.

   The new officers are Fran Pena, president; Harry Wong, treasurer; and Muriel Williams, secretary.

Use a dash

1. To show an abrupt change of thought.

   Invoice 76A—which is 10 days overdue—is for $670.

2. After a series to indicate a summarizing statement.

   Noisy fuel pump, worn rods, and failing brakes—for all these reasons I'm trading the car.

Use an exclamation point

After emphatic interjections or exclamatory sentences.

Terrific!   Hold it!   You bet!   What a great surprise!

APPENDIX C REFERENCE GUIDE

Capitalization

Capitalize:

1. First word of a sentence and of a direct quotation.

    We were tolerating instead of managing diversity. The speaker said, "We must value diversity, not merely recognize it."

2. Names of proper nouns—specific persons, places, or things.

    Common nouns: continent, river, car, street
    Proper nouns: Asia, Ohio, Buick, State Street.

3. Derivatives of proper nouns and geographical names.

    | American history | English accent |
    | German food | Ohio Valley |
    | Tampa, Florida | Mount Rushmore |

4. A personal or professional title when it precedes the name or a title of high distinction without a name.

    | Lieutenant Kahn | Mayor Walsh |
    | Doctor Welby | Mr. Ty Brooks |
    | Dr. Frank Collins | Miss Tate |
    | the President of the United States | |

5. Days of the week, months of the year, holidays, periods of history, and historic events.

    Monday, June 8   Labor Day   Renaissance

6. Specific parts of the country but not compass points that show direction.

    Midwest   the South   northwest of town

7. Family relationships when used with a person's name.

    Aunt Helen   my dad   Uncle John

8. Noun preceding a figure except for common nouns such as *line*, *page*, and *sentence*.

    Unit 1   Section 2   page 2   line 2

9. First and main words of side headings, titles of books, and works of art. Do not capitalize words of four or fewer letters that are conjunctions, prepositions, or articles.

    Computers in the News   *Raiders of the Lost Ark*

10. Names of organizations and specific departments within the writer's organization.

    Girl Scouts   our Sales Department

Number Expression

General guidelines

1. Use **words** for numbers *one* through *ten* unless the numbers are in a category with related larger numbers that are expressed as figures.

    He bought three acres of land. She took two acres. She wrote 12 stories and 2 plays in 13 years.

2. Use **words** for approximate numbers or large round numbers that can be expressed as one or two words. Use **numbers** for round numbers in millions or higher with their word modifier.

    We sent out about three hundred invitations. She contributed $3 million dollars.

3. Use **words** for numbers that begin a sentence.

    Six players were cut from the ten-member team.

4. Use **figures** for the larger of two adjacent numbers.

    We shipped six 24-ton engines.

Times and dates

5. Use **words** for numbers that precede o'clock (stated or implied).

    We shall meet from two until five o'clock.

6. Use **figures** for times with *a.m.* or *p.m.* and days when they follow the month.

    Her appointment is for 2:15 p.m. on July 26.

7. Use **ordinals** for the day when it precedes the month.

    The 10th of October is my anniversary.

Money, percentages, and fractions

8. Use **figures** for money amounts and percentages. Spell out *cents* and *percent* except in statistical copy.

    The 16 percent discount saved me $145; Bill, 95 cents.

9. Use **words** for fractions unless the fractions appear in combination with whole numbers.

    one-half of her lesson   5 1/2   18 3/4

Addresses

10. Use **words** for street names First through Tenth and **figures** or ordinals for streets above Tenth. Use **figures** for house numbers other than number **one**. (If street name is a number, separate it from house number with a dash.)

    One Lytle Place   Second Avenue
    142—53rd Street

APPENDIX C REFERENCE GUIDE

Spelling Rules

1. To make most nouns, plural, add *s*.

boy	boys
chair	chairs
parent	parents

2. Add *es* to nouns ending in *s, x, z, ch,* or *sh*.

Jones	Jones
tax	taxes
buzz	buzzes
church	churches
wish	wishes

3. If a noun ends in a consonant plus *y*, change the *y* to *i* and add *es*.

puppy	puppies
fly	flies

4. Add *es* to some nouns ending in a consonant plus *o*.

potato	potatoes
BUT not pianos	

5. For some nouns ending in *f* or *fe*, change the *f* or *fe* to *ves*.

Half	halves
Wolf	wolves

6. Memorize or look up irregular nouns.

child	children
woman	women

7. Keep a silent *e* before a suffix that begins with a consonant. Drop it before a suffix that begins with a vowel.

excite	excitement
excite	exciting

8. When adding a suffix that begins with a vowel to a word that ends with a vowel and consonant, double the consonant.

commit	commitment
shop	shopping

9. When you add a prefix, the spelling does not change.

wash	prewash
view	preview

10. Put *i* before *e* except after *c* or when the letters sound like *a*, as in *neighbor* and *weigh*.

receive	believe
neighbor	weigh

Composition

Most careers require good writing skills. You can learn to be an effective writer with practice. Writing at the keyboard facilitates editing and is easier and more effective than handwriting documents. Editing requires complete focus on each of the following areas:

Content accuracy—Determine what needs to be included in a message and then check to see that necessary information is included and that all information is accurate.

Organization—Check sentence structure to see that ideas are presented logically and flow smoothly.

Writing style—Ensure that the message is clear, crisp, concise, and written at an appropriate level.

Mechanical correctness—Check for errors in grammar, spelling, punctuation, capitalization, number usage, and word usage.

Composition Guides

1. Begin with short, easy sentences and paragraphs on topics in which you have knowledge. Then work on putting the sentences and paragraphs together for complete messages.
2. Key your thoughts first and then edit them carefully. It is very difficult to write perfect copy when you begin keying.
3. Use familiar words and a simple, straightforward writing style.
4. Edit to ensure that sentences are carefully arranged, clear, and grammatically correct.
5. Structure paragraphs carefully, making sure that all sentences in the paragraphs relate to the same topic and that they flow logically.
6. Edit and proofread carefully.

★ **TIP**

Editing and proofreading usually make the difference between high-quality and mediocre writing.

APPENDIX C REFERENCE GUIDE

Proofreading

Often the difference between high-quality and mediocre documents is in how carefully they are proofread. Careful proofreading ensures the accuracy of the final document.

Proofreading requires complete focus on each of the following areas:

Overall appearance of a document—check for appropriate stationery, attractive placement, and correct and consistent format.

Content accuracy—check for accuracy and completeness, such as making sure dates are correct and times are not left off.

Mechanical correctness—check for keying errors, as well as mistakes in spelling, grammar, punctuation, capitalization, word usage, and number usage. Review basic guides if you are not comfortable with your knowledge level in each of the areas listed.

Proofreading Guides

1. Check the document using the Spelling and Grammar commands.
2. Proofread the document on the screen slowly, on a word-by-word basis. Focus on words that may be spelled correctly but are misused, such as *you/your, is/in, if/it, there/their, two/to/too, then/than,* and *principle/principal.*
3. Check specifically for capitalization, punctuation, and number usage.
4. Check to see that the document is complete, ensuring that enclosure or copy notations are not left off.
5. Verify that each number is correct. The only way to ensure that a number is correct is to check it against the source from which it was keyed.
6. Preview the document on screen to ensure that placement is appropriate.
7. Print the document and proofread it again. It is helpful to use a guide (ruler, large envelope, or folded sheet of paper). Move it down line by line as you read. Mark the corrections using proofreaders' marks. Refer to a list of common proofreaders' marks found in the right column of this page.

> **TIP**
> Learn to proofread on the screen first and then, as a last check, proofread the printed document again.

Proofreading Statistical Copy

Statistical copy requires special attention. It is very easy to make errors in keying numbers, and it is very difficult to determine if a number keyed is correct.

The same thing is true for a date or time.

1. Verify numbers against the original source, verify dates against the calendar, and check computations with a calculator.
2. Read numbers in groups. For example, the telephone number 618.555.0123 can be read in three parts: *six-one-eight, five-five-five, zero-one-two-three.*
3. Read numbers aloud and preferably with a partner checking against the original copy.

> **TIP**
> An error in a number could have significant negative consequences; for example, keying $300,000 rather than $400,000 in quoting a price or authorizing a loan at 7% when the correct percentage is 8% could prove to be very costly.

Proofreaders' Marks

#	Add horizontal space
‖	Align
~~	Bold
Cap or ≡	Capitalize
[ ]	Center
⌒	Close up
⸜	Delete
∧	Insert
⌄ ⌄	Insert quotation marks
... or *stet*	Let it stand; ignore correction
/ or *lc*	Lowercase
⌐	Move left
¬	Move right
⌐⌐	Move up
⌐⌐	Move down
¶	Paragraph
sp	Spell out
∼ or *tr*	Transpose
___	italic or (ital)
wf	Wrong font

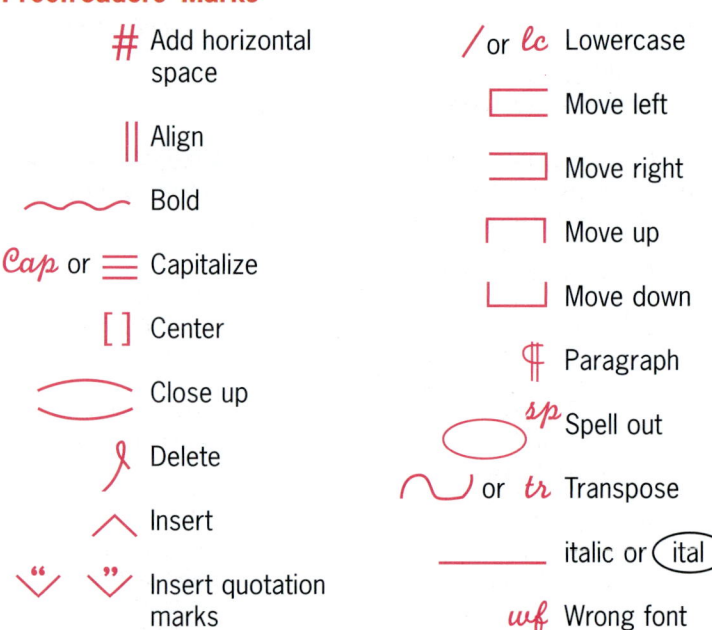

APPENDIX C REFERENCE GUIDE

Index

A
A, control of, 1-3
Abbreviations, spacing with, 1-40
Accountability, 1a-30
Alignment, 1a-10
Ampersand (&), control of, 1-59
And (&) sign. *See* Ampersand (&)
Apostrophe ('), control of, 1-25
Assessment, 1-64–1-65
Asterisk (*), control of, 1-61
At (@), control of, 1-61

B
B, control of, 1-18
Backspace key, control of, 1-58
Blogs, 1a-26
Bookmark, 1a-23, 1a-26
Bookmarking sites, 1a-26
Browser, 1a-23

C
C, control of, 1-15
Capitalization, 1a-11–1a-12
Caps lock, 1-30
Career success. *See* Workplace success
Civility, 1b-3
Cloud computing, 1a-22, 1a-24
Colon (:), control of, 1-59
Comma (,), control of, 1-17; usage, 1a-14
Communication, workplace, 1a-29
Communication skills, 1a-11–1a-22; capitalization, 1a-11–1a-12; commas, 1a-14; composition, 1a-20–1a-22; number expression, 1a-12–1a-13; pronoun agreement, 1a-14; pronoun case, 1a-13; proofreading, 1a-17–1a-20; spelling, 1a-16; subject-verb agreement, 1a-15
Composition, 1a-20–1a-22
Conceptual skills, 1a-27
Conversation, 1a-29
Copy, difficulty of, 1-32
Critical skills, 1a-27–1a-32. *See* Workplace Success
Critical thinking, 1a-28

D
D, control of, 1-3
Dash (—), 1-51

Decimal (.), 1-81
Decision making, 1a-28
Desktop computers, 1b-6
Digital citizenship, civility, 1b-3; misuse/abuse, 1b-2–1b-3; safety, 1b-3; technical literacy, 1b-2
Dollar sign ($), control of, 1-51
Dressing, 1a-29

E
E, control of, 1-7
Editing, 1-60, 1-62, 1-65
Eight (8), control of, 1-40
Email, Web-based, 1a-24–1a-25
Enter, 1-4
Equal sign (=), control of, 1-61
Exclamation point (!), control of, 1-55
Eye contact, 1a-29

F
F, control of, 1-3
Five (5), control of, 1-42
Format documents, 1a-8
Four (4), control of, 1-46

G
G, control of, 1-21
Google Docs, 1a-24
gwam (gross words a minute), 1-38–1-39

H
H, control of, 1-11
Handshake, 1a-29
Hard return, 1-4
High-frequency words, 1-41
Home-row position, 1-3
Hyphen (-), control of, 1-51

I
I, control of, 1-5
Identity theft, 1b-3
Information verification, 1b-2
Internet, 1a-23
Interview, 1a-31–1a-32

J
J, control of, 1-3

K
K, control of, 1-3
Keyboarding, value of, 1-5

L
L, control of, 1-3
Laptops, 1b-6
Left shift, control of, 1-11

M
M, control of, 1-24
Micro-blogging, 1a-26
Microsoft Office 365, 1a-24

N
N, control of, 1-7
New document, 1a-8
Nine (9), control of, 1-46
Number expression, 1a-12–1a-13
Number sign (#), 1-53
Numeric keypad, 1-77–1-82
NUMLOCK, 1-78

O
O, control of, 1-15
One (1), control of, 1-40
OneDrive, 1a-24–1a-25
Outlook.com, 1a-24

P
P, control of, 1-18
Paragraph formats, 1a-10
Parentheses ( ), control of, 1-57
Percent sign (%), control of, 1-55
Period (.), control of, 1-12
Photo sharing, 1a-26
Phrases, keying tips, 1-9–1-10
Piracy, 1b-3
Plagiarism, 1b-3
Plus sign (+), control of, 1-61
Posture, 1a-29
Pound symbol (#), control of, 1-53
Print, 1a-8
Privacy, 1b-3

Pronoun, agreement, 1a-14; case, 1a-13
Proofreaders' marks, 1-66, 1a-17
Proofreading, 1-65, 1a-17–1a-20

Q

Q, control of, 1-24
Question mark (?), control of, 1-21
Quotation mark ("), control of, 1-28

R

R, control of, 1-14
Right shift, control of, 1-14

S

S, control of, 1-3
Safety, 1b-3
Search engine, 1a-23
Seven (7), control of, 1-44
Six (6), control of, 1-48
Skill Builder, 1-35–1-39, 1-66–1-76
Skills: communication. *See* Communication skills; conceptual, 1a-27; soft. *See* Soft skills; technical, 1a-27
Slash (/), control of, 1-53
Social media, 1a-26
Social media tools, 1a-26
Social networks, 1a-26
Soft skills, 1a-27–1a-32; accountability, 1a-30; communication, 1a-29; critical thinking, 1a-28; decision making, 1a-28; definition, 1a-27; interview with follow-up activities, 1a-31–1a-32
Space Bar, 1-4

Spacing, with abbreviations, 1-40; with dash, 1-51; with dollar sign, 1-51; with percent sign, 1-55
Spelling, 1a-16
Subject-verb agreement, 1a-15

T

T, control of, 1-12
TAB key, 1-28
Tabs, Word Processor, 1a-9
Technical literacy, 1b-2
Technical skills, 1a-27
Technique Builder, drills, 1-35–1-39, 1-66–1-76
Technology, health issues, 1b-5; posture/position, 1b-6; work environment, 1b-6
Text formats, 1a-9
Three (3), control of, 1-48
Timed Writing feature, 1-38–1-39
Two (2), control of, 1-44

U

U, control of, 1-22
URL, 1a-23

V

V, control of, 1-25
Video sharing, 1a-26

W

W, control of, 1-17
Web-based computing, 1a-23–1a-26; cloud computing, 1a-24; Internet, 1a-23; social media, 1a-26; social media tools, 1a-26; Web-based email, 1a-24–1a-25

Web logs. *See* Blogs
Windows Start Screen, 1a-2
Word: blank document, 1a-3; blank document screen, 1a-4; close document, 1a-7; format document, 1a-8; managing files, 1a-5; new document, 1a-8; open existing, 1a-7; opening screen, 1a-3; paragraph format, 1a-10; print document, 1a-8; saving, 1a-6; text document, 1a-9
Word processing, 1a-2–1a-10
Work environment, 1b-6
Workplace success, 1a-27–1a-32; conceptual skills, 1a-27; soft skills. *See* Soft skills; technical skills, 1a-27

X

X, control of, 1-22

Y

Y, control of, 1-27

Z

Z, control of, 1-27
Zero (0), control of, 1-42